THE ULTIMATE GUIDE TO
CLASSROOM
PUBLISHING

Judy Green

Pembroke Publishers Limited

To Sharon Brain,
for welcoming me into the world of books
and making it fun along the way

© 1999   Pembroke Publishers
538 Hood Road
Markham, Ontario, Canada L3R 3K9
www.pembrokepublishers.com

Distributed in the U.S. by Stenhouse Publishers
P.O. Box 360
York, Maine 03909
www.stenhouse.com

Pembroke Publishers gratefully acknowledges the support of the Department
of Canadian Heritage.

Canadian Cataloguing in Publication Data

Green, Judy, 1958–
    The ultimate guide to classroom publishing

ISBN 1-55138-112-5

1. English language – Composition and exercises – Study and teaching
(Elementary). 2. Publishers and Publishing – Study and teaching
(Elementary). 3. Children – Writing. I. Title.

LB1576.G745 1999   372.62'3   C99-931403-3

Cover Design: John Zehethofer
Cover Photography: Ajay Photographics
Typesetting: JayTee Graphics

Printed and bound in Canada
9 8 7 6 5 4 3 2 1

Contents

Preface

As a child, I loved books. My mother read to me all the time. Every Saturday we loaded up at the library with a pile of books. I grew up in the 1960s with stories that I still remember vividly. *The Story about Ping* was a favorite, followed by Beverly Cleary's novels. Often, I would read well past bedtime, and scramble to turn out the light as I heard my father's footsteps coming down the hall. I can still recall trying to decipher Nancy Drew mysteries in the dark!

Luckily, in our household, there was all sorts of stuff to read. I read everything I could lay my hands on. Also, very importantly, I often heard people reading aloud. *I'm convinced that I learnt how to write mostly through reading.*

At school they taught us to read with Dick and Jane. We read stories from a grey book every day, and then answered ten comprehension questions in our notebooks. After that we turned to the reading lab, and worked our way through color-coded stories with self-marking question cards. We were oblivious to authors and illustrators, or anything to do with *publishing*.

Kids today have a much broader literary base. They talk about books they love, and of writers they are familiar with. Whenever I ask kids how many of them *like* to read, their eyes light up! When I ask kids who their favorite authors are, they give brilliant replies:

"C.S. Lewis!"
"Gordon Korman!"
"Robert Munsch!"
"Judy Blume!"
"Roald Dahl!"

And many more. They tell me what books they like best by these authors, and why. And whenever I ask children how many of them like to draw, or would like to be a book illustrator, the response is overwhelming!

There are, of course, several reasons for their bubbling enthusiasm. One is the shift towards literature-based programs in today's elementary schools. Teachers do remarkable things to motivate kids in reading and writing — they set up publishing programs, conduct author studies, invite professionals in from the book business, organize Young Authors Conferences, host Family Reading Nights, and plan all sorts of exciting activities to celebrate Children's Book Week. Such efforts help students make the reading/writing connection.

Teachers today view writing as a *process* that develops along with other language skills, especially reading. They give their students opportunities to write for various purposes and to master various parts of the process — such as how to generate ideas, create a plan, write a first draft, edit, and use visual elements to enhance their work. Now, many schools are equipped with laminating and cerlox-binding machines, computers, color printers, and scanners as part of the "publishing" process.

As well, more parents today realize that reading is a key element to school success. In a *Maclean's* magazine cover story called "The KidLit Boom," journalist Diane Turbide has described the growth of children's book publishing, attributing it to "the market of baby boomers with money to spend on their kids, and a recognition on the role of books in raising bright, imaginative children."

The children's book industry has blossomed in the last three decades. Before the 1970s, only a handful of full-color books were published. Authors such as Jean Little and Robert McCloskey were writing as early as the 1950s, but most books back then had black-and-white illustrations, unappealing covers, and hardly any promotion.

Today, happily, the state of children's books has changed dramatically. The sophistication of the product has grown in every way. We see good covers, illustrations by talented artists, infrastructures for promoting children's books, many book awards, and more publicity. There is a glorious feast of choice. Hundreds of new children's books are published each year and they are better — funnier, deeper, and more visually appealing than ever. From that point of view, it's an exciting time to be in the teaching profession!

After teaching elementary school, I worked as a Book Club editor at Scholastic Canada. Teachers often called to ask if we could visit their schools to talk to their students about publishing. Working to deadlines, I did not always find this possible, but occasionally I would pack some materials and go.

One day, after my son was born and I had begun freelance writing and editing, a teacher friend invited me to give a talk at her school. She said her Grade 5 students had been doing a lot of author studies, *loved* books, and were keen to publish their own work. Several authors and illustrators graciously loaned me some of their original materials; I gave the kids some writing, editing, and illustrations ideas, and built upon that. Since then, I've visited more than 500 schools and conducted many professional development workshops on publishing. Everywhere, people are keen on the books and authors we discuss!

One thing is clear: children *love* to learn about their favorite authors. It's important to look at how writers are created because it relates to reading. Authors and illustrators are powerful role models. Inevitably, as I am ready to leave a school, a minor miracle occurs: some students (often boys) approach me shyly. "When I grow up," they say, "I want to draw and write books too."

What could be more rewarding?

Introduction: Nurturing Creativity

Besides being a book hound as a child, I constantly wrote letters and stories of my own. By high school, though, I had lost all interest in books, and began struggling in nearly every subject. I almost quit Economics when the teacher assigned a writing project. How could I write about a topic so confusing to me, and one I knew so little about?

Rescue efforts by my father led to a brainwave: I would write a primer about economics! The result was "Popping Corn into Money," a fanciful tale about a boy who wants enough money to buy a skateboard interwoven with a series of basic economic principles. My sister brought the story to life with comic illustrations.

We completed the book in about three weeks. I had to read other books about economics and question things I did not understand. I had to edit for correct language and collaborate with my father and sister. We did lots of thinking, talking, changing, rearranging the text and illustrations to get them right. What a thrill to discover that I could be an author, get an A+ for the final product, and not fail Economics!

Now, my book is a treasure to me. It is the only work I kept from all my school years, a reminder of what can happen when I choose to be creative. Creativity involves hard work, risk taking, and determination. My book is a token of the encouragement my father always gave me. He said that anything is possible, that we all have the ability to turn our dreams into realities. Now, in my life's work, I have the chance to pass that encouragement on . . .

Creativity is at the core of a child's ability to compete. It is not a feel-good experience, but a capability that must be nurtured every day, in every interaction; not a sprinkling of isolated epiphanies, but a process that unfolds — or sadly, doesn't unfold — in classrooms every day.

When I visit schools and speak at Young Authors Conferences, I meet all kinds of kids who have made their own books. Watching them share their work moves me! It reinforces everything I believe about creativity. I admire these children for having the courage to turn ideas into masterpieces, and love looking at their books. I can see the light in their eyes as they turn the pages. I know they are experiencing the thrill of discovering the creative genius that lives in each of them.

From all that I've seen, kids are excited about reading, writing, and illustration. They look up to the experts who make books. Today's children are lucky to have so many great books to read. Still, you don't see this kind of enthusiasm without the hard work of energetic and caring people. In the past few years, I have met terrific teachers who work tirelessly to make books come alive for their students.

More than an isolated activity then, publishing is part of an integrated program. It includes book-sharing opportunities, author studies, interactive hall and wall displays, student reference materials, parent involvement, and celebrations. These are the driving forces towards motivation.

Yet when it comes to publishing, some teachers admit that "they haven't done any of that yet." Some teachers blanch when you mention publishing. They see it as intimidating, time-consuming, and a lot of work. Yes, it involves work (ask any author or illustrator to tell you differently!), but the positive effects of publishing are worth it at all levels.

This book is organized into two parts, Paving the Way for Publishing and Publishing in the Classroom. Here's an overview of what you'll find.

Part A suggests ideas for planning an author study and activities that can be used to explore books. You'll find engaging activities that link reading and writing, and ideas to inspire students in their own publishing projects. Also in Part A, you and your students "meet" author and illustrator Barbara Reid. Beyond information about her, there are suggestions for studying her illustration style and for encouraging children to explore her techniques in their own artwork.

Part B explores publishing in depth from start to finish, including getting writing ideas, editing, illustrating, designing, binding, and sharing. Fresh insights from many popular children's book creators will spark interest by students in their own work. In addition to special ways for celebrating the finished product, Publishing in the Classroom contains resource lists, evaluation techniques, and career information for budding writers and illustrators.

A teacher's role in the publishing process is similar to that of an editor — nurturer, supporter, prodder, and prompter. You are also there to model the process — to demonstrate for your students how to read, write, proofread, illustrate, and talk about stories. Set them up for success! Create an emotional place for your young authors and illustrators to be brave in . . . to have their trust as you explore the process together.

As teachers, we want to create conditions that help children release that which lies waiting within them so that they can express themselves in bright colors, like a rainbow in the sky.

Part A

Paving the Way for Publishing

1

Begin with the Basics: Reading the Best Books

"Read a lot!" authors advise kids who want to be writers. "Reading is the key to writing. You can become better artists too." As a teacher, you play a key role in making sure that children grow as readers and writers. Our media-filled society provides other options for information and entertainment, but there is no more important way to help students learn to read and write than to share good books with them daily.

You can set the stage for publishing by exploring lots of books together. Books show your children that other people share the same worries as they do. They talk about the human condition, and deal with themes that touch all of us. Books also impart wisdom and bring great joy to our lives. Nothing is more exciting than a teacher of any grade sharing a good book with their class. No child — or adult — is too old to be read to.

Reading good books together also helps children learn how stories *work*. They hear the rhythms, listen to the words, get excited by the plots, and come to realize what makes effective beginnings and satisfying endings. Books help children develop their language skills. They also stir the imagination and stimulate many creative possibilities.

Picture books, by the way, are meant for people of all ages, not just children! They are a literary art form which appeals to a wide audience — children and adults. Some picture books have highly sophisticated artwork and are better suited for older students. Take time to talk about the illustrations you see in books. Examining artwork stimulates discussion at all grade levels. If you teach older students, encourage them to read picture books plus fiction, poetry, and non-fiction.

As often as you can, encourage students to express their creative talents. Look for writing and illustration opportunities in every activity and in every discipline. For example, if you are studying urban communities in social studies, students can write "city poems" or "observations on city life" with skyline paintings. To get to know your students in

Use Books as Models

Published books provide excellent teaching models. Use them to teach all the skills involved in publishing such as how to generate great story beginnings, create a sense of drama, design covers, incorporate a variety of illustrations, develop page layouts, and create borders. Encourage children to examine the art and writing in books, then apply the knowledge to their own work.

Not Just for Children Anymore!

In 1997, the Children's Book Council published the first *Not Just for Children Anymore!* catalogue celebrating the fact that even adults love children's books. This guide allows adults to share their enthusiasm for innovative children's publishing and includes a Classics category, with perennial favorites of childhood. (For more information, see page 40.)

Too Good to Miss is a list of outstanding Canadian children's books — classics, picture books, fiction, folk tales, poetry, history, and science — that no school should be without. *Too Good to Miss* is available from The Canadian Children's Book Centre. (See page 39 for information.)

September, ask them to write "me-poems" or "autobiographies" with body outlines, or face silhouettes, or personal collages. If an author visits your school, appoint students to write directions, introductions, and thank-yous, as well as draw maps on how to get there. Life's experiences stir responses that words and pictures can express.

How to Build an Environment in Which Creativity Flourishes

- Read to your students and talk about books every day.
- Model reading by having your students see you read during personal reading time; model writing for them, too.
- Display a variety of reading materials attractively around the room.
- Use authors and illustrators as role models for writing and illustration.
- Inspire students to publish their own material for others to read, and celebrate their creativity.
- Ensure that students have access to materials that relate to their own creativity.
- Invite parents to participate in publishing activities.

Building a Classroom Book Display

Be sure to expose your students to many different types of books. Give them plenty to choose from a variety of genres — fiction, poetry, non-fiction, and picture books. Hundreds of beautiful, original, *quality* children's books are published every year. Supply your students with good books by their favorite authors and illustrators. Books provide brilliant models for writing and illustrating techniques.

Try to show your students the *best* children's books: books that are well written and imaginatively illustrated. Choose from lists of award winners and recommended titles, because these books are acknowledged as the best children's literature. As often as possible, set high standards for your students. Plenty of great new books come out every year, as well as plenty of schlock. Pick great books to read with your students!

Librarian advice

Teacher-librarians are at the heart of promoting children's reading and writing. Many work endlessly to highlight books, arrange for author visits, and keep classroom teachers informed of the new titles. Often, students go to the library only when their teachers drop them off. Good teachers take their students to the library and spend time there getting to know how they can use books, magazines, and software to foster creativity in the classroom. Knowledgeable librarians, both in the school and at the public library, can help you choose the best children's books.

Writers need continual nourishment from the books of other writers. Help your students find good books outside of the classroom.

- Early in the school year, take your students to the school or public library. Reinforce their ability to use the library by explaining its rules and the reasons for them.
- Demonstrate the use of the computer or card catalogue and show the locations of the different categories of books.
- Explain how to use reference books such as dictionaries, atlases, and encyclopedias.
- Show your students how to open a new book and care for all books.

Remember! Expose your students to diverse reading materials to help them become versatile writers.

Newspapers, book clubs, and magazines

Many teachers keep up-to-date on current titles through book clubs (such as Scholastic and Troll). Monthly newsletters highlight the award winners and offer exciting teaching tips. Look for new titles each month and add quality books to your shelves. Build your classroom library with theme packs and reference titles specially selected for the curriculum. Book clubs can help you make good choices, and are a great way to enrich your classroom library.

Book reviewers in the media also help you select titles. With the ever-increasing quality, quantity, and variety of children's books, there is no shortage of books to review today. Many reviewers are subject to space and (in radio) time constraints, which forces them to concentrate on books they like rather than ones they don't.

The Internet

All the latest news in the world of children's books is available on-line. Many Web sites are meant for teachers, at primary through senior levels. You can visit the sites of book experts, get a sneak peek at publishers' anticipated bestsellers, and contact organizations for lists of award winners.

The following sites may be helpful for choosing children's books.

- *The Canadian Children's Book Centre*:
  www3.sympatico.ca/ccbc
  This site offers lists of children's book award-winners, tips from creators, advice on how to get published, information about Book Week, "book talk," and more.
- *CBC Online*:
  http://www.cbcbooks.org/navigation/teachers.html
  The Web site of the Children's Book Council in the United States includes children's book news, author and illustrator links, bibliographies, exciting reading activities, and more.
- *How Novel!*:
  http://strobe.lights.com/novel/welcome.html
  This site offers information on young adult literature. Resources include cover art, annotations, reviews, and publisher information for hundreds of novels, plus author photographs and biographies.
- *CM (Canadian Review of Materials)*:
  http://www.umanitoba.ca/cm/ home/about.html
  An electronic reviewing journal, *CM* reviews books, videos, audiotapes, and CD-ROMS produced for young people. It also publishes news, feature articles, interviews and Web reviews.
- *Internet Book Information Centre, Inc.*:
  http://sunsite.unc.edu/ibic/IBIC-homepage.html
  Here is a great site for booklovers, with links to many others.
- *The Looking Glass*:
  http://www.fis.utororonto.ca/~easun/looking_glass/about.html
  This electronic journal about Kid Lit features a variety of columns,

facets of illustration and design, insights from authors and illustrators, and more.

- *221B Baker Street*:
  http://members.tripod.com/~msherman/holmes.html
  Good readers will enjoy the adventures of Sherlock Holmes.
- *Online Children's Stories*:
  http://www.ucalgary.ca/~dkbrown/stories.html
  Take your students on a virtual class trip. Once there, they can read or download stories, send stories, and more!

Guides to new children's books

Guides to new children's books are produced annually and will help you in the selection process. They recommend a mix of simple and complex books for girls and boys, plus an assortment for every age and interest.

- *Canadian Book Review Annual's Canadian Children's Literature* reviews hundreds of books published annually. Each review contains a book summary, a rating of quality, price, and more. The annual includes a subject/author/title index and an overview of what's new for young readers. To order, call (416) 961-8537 or 1-888-463-7083. You can also visit the Web site: www.interlog.com/~cbra
- *Our Choice* recommends the best new Canadian children's books, videos, audiotapes, and CD-ROMs every year. To order, contact The Canadian Children's Book Centre:
  phone: (416) 975-0010; fax: (416) 975-1830;
  e-mail: ccbc@sympatico.ca; Web site: www3.sympatico.ca.ccbc
- *La Sélection de livres pour enfants et adolescents* is an annual guide to the best new French-Canadian children's books. To order, contact Communication-Jeunesse:
  phone: (514) 273-8167; fax: (514) 271-6812;
  Web site: http://pages.infinit.net/livrocj
- *Read Up on It!* is an annual kit which is based on a different theme each year. Besides an annotated list of books, it includes a poster and bookmarks. To order:
  phone (613) 995-7969; fax: (613) 991-9871;
  e-mail: publications@nlc-bnc.ca; Web site: www.nlc-bnc.ca/ruoi

Treasuries of recommended reading

Invaluable resource books such as the following will help you choose good books for children.

- *Everybody's Favourites*, by Arlene Perly Rae
- *The Reading Solution*, by Paul Kropp
- *Choosing Children's Books*, by David Booth, Larry Swartz, and Meguido Zola
- *Better Books! Better Readers!*, by Linda Hart-Hewins and Jan Wells

Updating Your Book Display

Once you've got plenty of good books in your room, keep reading interest high by changing the book display frequently. Make sure that it is always fresh. Every week or two, borrow new books from your library, and add seasonal titles to the mix. This doesn't take much work, but if your time is limited, maybe parent volunteers, senior students, or your own students can help.

One of the best teachers I know goes to the library every Friday afternoon after her students are dismissed, gets an assortment of about thirty books and displays them along the blackboard ledges around the room. The students arrive every Monday morning to find numerous new books — a feast for the eyes and mind!

Enlist student helpers to go to the library every week and get new books for the class. As a group, discuss important things to consider when picking good books. Teach them how to display them in your room and talk about them to their classmates. They will have input towards their own learning and see that you trust their ability to make good choices.

Periodically, check that the books on your shelves are in reasonable condition. Discovering that a book is incomplete can be distressing. Once, when my son and I were immersed in *The Magic School Bus on the Ocean Floor*, his "Home Reading" book, we found a huge chunk of pages gone! Sadly, our voyage was over. Please weed out books with missing pages.

Consider these guidelines when gathering books to display in your classroom:

- ❏ simple and more difficult books for girls and boys;
- ❏ an assortment for every interest;
- ❏ picture books, fiction, poetry, and non-fiction;
- ❏ interesting content and good illustrations;
- ❏ favorite authors and illustrators;
- ❏ award winners and recommended titles;
- ❏ seasonal titles and thematic tie-ins.

Giving Book Talks

At the beginning of the year, model for your students how to give an enthusiastic book talk. Choose one book from your display, and fire kids up about it! Describe the story, setting, theme, characters, and any special features (e.g., awards) about the book. Tell what you can about the author and illustrator, and identify other books by the same person. Read a passage to give your students a sense of the book.

Book talks need not take a lot of time or preparation. Some teachers make them part of morning exercises. Occasionally, you can invite guests, such as administrators or parents, in to give a book talk. Kids clamor for books other people have recommended enthusiastically.

After you have provided a few demonstrations, invite students to give their own book talks. They may opt to work with a partner — some kids panic in front of a crowd — or individually. Each day, ask a different volunteer to recommend a book, ensuring that every student will have several opportunities to share titles throughout the year. Using this approach, you can assess their reading and speaking abilities, interests, and group behavior, and your students will gain valuable experience in facing an audience.

Writing Book Blurbs

Kids can contribute to a class book of recommended reading. Whenever your students read a really great book — one that they'd like to recommend to others — invite them to write a blurb about it. The blurb should offer just enough information to attract other readers without giving away too many details. Encourage students to make illustrations that will help bring their descriptions to life. Other children can read the recommendations to choose new books.

This chapter has emphasized the importance of reading the "best" books because these provide excellent models for writing and spur creativity. It's probably true that people write the kind of stories they like to read and are most influenced by what they enjoy. However, reading anything, whether a critic has judged it good or not, is a valid start. You want to get kids excited about books, eager to explore the library, discover a dynamic new author, and open the pages of an engrossing story. Use all the creative ways you can to turn on your students to reading.

2

Making the Reading/Writing Connection

"Genre reading can be a helpful tool for children to explore, compare, describe, and assess types of books and various forms of writing. Knowing the characteristics of a genre can help children to model it in their writing."

— David Booth, in *Guiding the Reading Process*

As a teacher, you know that reading sparks writing, which in turn leads to a more sophisticated understanding of reading. You realize that writing and reading are part of a continuum — one feeds into the other. If this is so, where do you start?

We begin to build awareness of the reading/writing connection in Kindergarten when a child tells us a story and we write it down so the child can read it back to us. As our students get older, stimulating the reading/writing continuum becomes more challenging. If students are to broaden their range of skills, we needs lots of exciting approaches.

Kids can use published books as models to create their own books. They can write, edit, and illustrate stories, as well as include information about the author and illustrator, a dedication, and a table of contents. Some may even design fancy borders and endpapers for their books.

As often as possible, we should allow children to read from and respond to each other's work. Presenting their own work provides children with a purpose for writing. An audience provides motivation.

When kids first see themselves as authors, they begin to look more critically at books. They become aware of the authors behind the books they read, and aspire to new levels of sophistication in their own work. They realize that books are the result of a process which includes developing ideas, writing, and revising drafts. They become "insiders" in the reading/writing process.

Introductory Activities: All about Books

Before professional authors and illustrators plunge into a new book project, they will often devote time to familiarizing themselves with particular genres, themes, and/or topics. For example, when award-winning author/

Teach your students to view books as something very special. Use published books to point out outside parts of a book, such as cover, title, author's name, and illustrator's name. Show them, too, key inside parts of a book, such as table of contents, chapters, glossary, endpapers, author pages, and index.

Understanding the parts of a book will help children when they design books of their own.

These definitions are largely based on Harry Shaw's *Dictionary of Literary Terms* (New York: McGraw Hill, 1972).

illustrator Barbara Reid wanted to write and illustrate her own fairy tale, she spent months at the library, studying lots of models. A person cannot simply sit down and wait for great ideas to miraculously come.

Likewise, children need to explore books and get acquainted with the publishing process before they write and illustrate their own books. We must devote time to some introductory activities. Through these, students will discover aspects of books that they may not have thought about before and get ideas to feed their own creativity. Remember, we want them to see many possibilities!

Understanding Types of Books

Develop a reference chart of types of books, such as picture books, fiction, non-fiction, and poetry, and then ask students, as a large group, to classify books in your classroom according to the chart. Or, gather together a random sampling of books and show ways of sorting them.

Classifying books by their form, or genre, helps children realize how many different kinds of stories exist; however, classifying can be challenging. As Sandy Asher, editor of *But That's Another Story*, explains: "The most significant elements of a story decide its genre. But not all stories fit neatly into one category." Encourage your students to look for the main focus of the books they are classifying.

After students sort and classify a large collection of books, you may wish to extend the activity by studying various genres. Open the gates to non-fiction, for instance. At one time, most non-fiction books were painfully dull. Today, thanks to innovative writers such as Linda Granfield and Ruth Heller, children can read non-fiction books that are just as imaginative as favorite storybooks.

Don't overlook non-fiction

Encourage students to read and write non-fiction. For example, with *Boondoggle*, by Camilla Gryski, as a model, they can make their own how-to books. Just as *Boondoggle* gives instructions on making bracelets woven with plastic lace and embroidery thread, kids can make their own how-to books by writing about something they are good at and adding complementary pictures.

Help students understand what non-fiction is, giving examples. Here are a few key characteristics:

- You can start reading anywhere in the book — you don't have to begin at the beginning to gain meaning.
- Information is found in the headings, the captions, the illustrations, and the written text.
- The words and pictures work together to help you determine greater meaning.
- A table of contents can direct you to specific information.

These definitions are largely based on Harry Shaw's *Dictionary of Literary Terms* (New York: McGraw Hill, 1972).

Common Book Genres

fiction fashioned to entertain and instruct. Its main purpose is to make readers *feel*.

non-fiction presents ideas based on facts and reality

science fiction explores possibilities across time and space. A story that *could* happen

fairy tale a story about elves, dragons, sprites, and other magical creatures. These "spirits" usually have mischievous temperaments, wisdom, and power to control people however they choose.

folk tale fanciful yarn handed down from one generation to the next; wit and wisdom intact. All have been passed down orally — as spoken stories — before being written down.

humor looks at everyday events in a lighthearted way

adventure stories unfamiliar places and unexpected danger. Characters must use their strength to find their way back to safety.

suspense real places, realistic characters, but the reader never knows what will happen next

detective stories depend on a detective who solves a crime logically and systematically

animal stories can be about animals that think and talk as human beings do, or about those that do not

historical fiction a realistic story set in the past. Events and settings are based on fact. Characters and plot are either real or invented.

time-travel fantasy magic or mishap allows characters to slip out of their day-to-day lives and experience adventures in a different time and place. A story that could never happen

horror stories based on happenings we hope never come true. They put us as close to peril as we care to go. Thrills, chills and a touch of mystery

poetry metrical form, patterned language, or rhythmical composition designed to produce pleasure through beautiful, imaginative or profound thoughts

biography a form of non-fiction in which the subject is the life of an individual

autobiography a form of non-fiction in which the author recounts his or her own history

picture book a story in which the author's text and illustrator's pictures have equal importance

Some exciting examples of non-fiction are listed below. Note how the titles spark interest.

- *The Amazing Dirt Book*, by Paulette Bourgeois
- *Champion Defencemen*, by James Duplacey
- *Crime Science*, by Vivien Bowers
- *Electric Gadgets and Gizmos*, by Alan Bartholomew
- *The Kids Cottage Games Book*, by Jane Drake and Ann Love
- *Newest and Coolest Dinosaurs*, by Phil Currie and Colleayn O. Mastin

Seeing the appeal of picture books

Some of the world's best modern art isn't hanging on a museum wall — it's in children's books. Hundreds of gifted artists are making magnificent picture books with everything from colorful swirls of paint to Plasticine.

Picture books are meant for people of all ages. Some are simple in nature, like the award-winning *A Child's Treasury of Nursery Rhymes* by Kady MacDonald Denton. Others are quite complex, such as Graeme Base's *Animalia* or *The Eleventh Hour*. Picture books provide a fantastic framework for your writing and art programs. Use them from Kindergarten to Grade 8. (See Chapter 12, Looking at Book Illustration, for more information about the value of picture books.)

Studying story structure

Understanding the parts of a story is important when children read and write stories of their own. Help students examine story elements with the following activities.

- To show what they know about a story character, tell children to make a character-sketch web. Ask them to draw a picture of the character in the centre of a piece of paper. Then, around the picture, they can jot down facts about the character. For example, a child who has read Beverly Cleary's *Ramona the Brave* might note that Ramona wants to be brave, but is sometimes a pest.
- Make a class chart that summarizes characters, setting, plot, problem, and solution. For example, a chart for E.B. White's story, *Charlotte's Web*, might look like this:

Charlotte's Web

Characters	Plot	Setting	Problem	Solution
Wilbur the pig Fern Charlotte the spider	Wilbur is lonely until he makes friends with Charlotte.	spring/farm	Charlotte does not want Wilbur to be killed by the farmer.	Charlotte thinks of a plan to save Wilbur's life.

At the end of an author study, your class could have one big chart, treating several books by the same author in the manner above.

- Have children write or draw about story elements by making a flip book, as follows:
  1. Fold lightly colored construction paper 30 cm x 46 cm (12 in. x 18 in.) in half lengthwise.
  2. Make four evenly spaced cuts in the top half (9 cm or 3.6 in. apart) to make five flaps.
  3. Label the flaps with the story elements and have children draw or write about each category underneath the flaps.

Many Grade 7 and 8 teachers do Picture Book Units with their students. Because the picture book story is short, but requires all the skills of a longer story, this process makes an ideal classroom publishing project. First, spend several days reading good picture books together. Then brainstorm story ideas together and begin writing. Try to give your students lots of time (at least 6 to 8 weeks) for creativity. After your class has finished publishing their own picture books, arrange for them to share their stories with a Kindergarten or Grade 1 class.

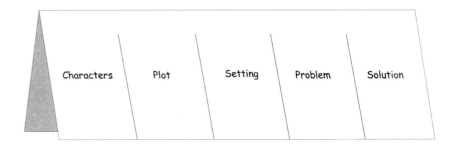

Making a 10 best books list

Another way in which kids can look at books critically is to ask them to write their own list of best children's books. They learn what qualities make a good book, and can apply this understanding to their own publishing projects. They may divide their list any way they like: they can choose ten best picture books, ten best novels, or ten best non-fiction books. How to choose? Have them keep these points in mind:

- What gives the book lasting value?
- Are there pictures that should be considered? Students should look at the illustrations as well as the writing in evaluating the strength of a book.

Encouraging Students to See Themselves as Authors

Once students have looked at books, invite them to think more about the people behind them. If you teach young children, ask them what we call someone who writes a story. Explain that an author is someone who writes books for others to read. Some authors write about things from their childhood, or people they know. Others write about topics that interest them, such as sports, planets, history, or art. Authors often do more than write books. Some also teach, some are mothers or fathers, and some are children.

Then ask your children whether they consider themselves authors. Chances are, they will say no. Some may say they're "just kids"; others will say they've "never made a book before." Assure your students that if they have ever written a story, they are authors too!

Lead children to talk about what they do when they are authors. Encourage them to bring their own experiences into the discussion and develop a reference chart similar to the one below.

What Student Authors Do

1. Think of ideas.
2. Make lists.
3. Write outlines.
4. Start to write.
5. Share your story with friends.
6. Show it to the teacher.
7. Revise your story.

What Do Authors Do?, by Eileen Christelow, will provide your students with a wonderful introduction to the publishing process. You might use it to make an effective bulletin-board display. You might read the book to your students, then summarize main ideas on large cards for the wall.

What do authors do?

Brainstorm ideas→ Make lists or outlines→ Start to write→ Share stories→ Take a break→ Write again→ Manuscript is sent to the publisher→ Author works with an editor→ Finish any illustrations→ Write dedication→ Take author photo→ Book is printed and sent to warehouses→ Celebrate!→ Magazines and newspapers review book→ Author visits schools, libraries and bookstores→ Author thinks of ideas for next book!

There are several active measures you can take to help children see themselves as authors.

Author of the Week centre

Establish a bulletin board or display table which features a different student-writer each week. Show a picture of the student-writer, an autobiography, and work samples (pictures, stories, published books, poems, etc.).

Author profiles

Ask students, in pairs, to interview one another about themselves as writers. Before they begin their interviews, have them make up a list of questions to ask. For example:

What stories have you written?	Who are your favorite authors?
Which one is your favorite? Why?	What do you do in your spare time?
Where do your ideas come from?	What would you like to write in
How do you like writing?	the future?

Getting a Glimpse into the Publishing Process

For a fresh and funny look at how authors write books and get them published, read: *What Do Authors Do?*, by Eileen Christelow (Kindergarten to Grade 3; ages 5 to 8).

"Dialogue in cartoon balloons and brief text describe the writing process and the mechanics of publishing. . . . Young readers will appreciate the determination, patience and hard work it takes to produce the books they enjoy and will welcome the journey from idea to finished book."

— *School Library Journal,* starred

Picture Book Partnerships

In *Writing Picture Books: What Works and What Doesn't*, Kathy Stinson describes steps of writing picture books, from character and plot development to humor, suspense, and fantasy. She suggests forming writing partnerships (writing buddies) between Grade 7 or 8 students and children from a primary class. After the older students interview the younger students, they can create a story together. The older student writes the story and tests it both on his writing buddy, and against Stinson's criteria.

Author's chair

Designate a special chair where students can sit when they read their published work to classmates. You might use a rocking chair, a cushion, a stool, or an attractively labelled chair. Put the chair in your group meeting area. When a student publishes a story, invite him or her to sit in the author's chair and share it with the class. Keep in mind that not all students will choose to share their published stories this way. If they do, give them an opportunity to rehearse the reading before presenting to the entire class. Focus your observations on the child's expression, intonation, phrasing, fluency, and self-esteem.

Providing an author's chair has several benefits:

- It encourages students to publish.
- It provides an audience for the student.
- It celebrates students' published work.
- It instils a feeling of authorship.

You can also help students see themselves as authors in the following ways:

✓ Conduct author studies.
✓ Invite a professional from the book business to address your class.
✓ Set up a publishing program.
✓ Celebrate your students' writing with a special event.

These ways are explored further in later chapters.

FEATURE: Gordon Korman — A Professional Author since Childhood

One has only to look at the proliferation of Gordon Korman books to appreciate why he is a great inspiration to budding writers. Gordon Korman published his first book when he was only fourteen years old! Since then he has written dozens of hilarious novels — including the ever popular *Bruno and Boots* series. If your students are reading chapter books, invite them to list books they know by Gordon Korman. Here are some titles:

This Can't Be Happening at Macdonald Hall	*Radio Fifth Grade*
Something Fishy at Macdonald Hall	*The Twinkie Squad*
Macdonald Hall Goes Hollywood	*The Toilet Paper Tigers*
Beware the Fish!	*The 6th Grade Nickname Game*
I Want to Go Home	*The Chicken Doesn't Skate*
Who Is Bugs Potter?	

Gordon Korman grew up in Thornhill, Ontario. When he was in Grade 7, his teacher asked the class to write novels. They had to hand in one chapter every week. Gordon Korman made up a story about two boys named Bruno and Boots who go to a private school called Macdonald

Hall. Just for fun, Gordon sent his story to a publishing company and he became one of Canada's youngest authors. He was *twelve* when he wrote *This Can't Be Happening at Macdonald Hall* and fourteen when the book came out. By the time he had finished high school, Korman had five books published already! Now, he's written more than twenty books for kids.

Most of Gordon Korman's books are best suited for kids in Grades 4 to 6. As Korman grew older, he started writing for an older audience. Some of these books are *Losing Joe's Place, Son of Interflux,* and *Life in the Semester of a Garbage Bag. Liar, Liar, Pants on Fire* is a fun-filled chapter book accompanied by whimsical illustrations, ideal for third graders. Korman has even published books of poetry, such as *The D-Poems of Jeremy Bloom,* and *The Last-Place Sports Poems of Jeremy Bloom* which he co-authored with his mother, Bernice Korman.

Many of Gordon Korman's books are translated into other languages — French, Swedish, Danish, Norwegian, and Chinese. Kids all over the world can read his books. "Translation makes for some neat situations," Korman says. "In the Bruno and Boots books, the headmaster of Macdonald Hall is Mr. Sturgeon — his nickname is 'The Fish.' In French the nickname becomes 'Caviar.'

"There's the scene where Miss Scrimmage, thinking that she's protecting the students of Miss Scrimmage's Finishing School for Young Ladies [across the road from Macdonald Hall], accidentally fires her shotgun into the sign in front of her school. The blast blows the letters '*n*' and '*i*' out of the word 'finishing.' The sign now says: 'Miss Scrimmage's Fishing School for Young Ladies.' See? It doesn't translate into any other language, and had to be left out of foreign editions."

Gordon Korman gets a lot of mail from his readers. Often it leads to new writing ideas. When kids used to ask him to write a story about baseball, he would reply, "If the Toronto Blue Jays ever win a World Series I *will* write a baseball story!" So in 1992, when the Blue Jays won the World Series the first time, Gordon Korman wrote *The Toilet Paper Tigers.* It's about a boys baseball team with a girl coach, sponsored by a local toilet paper company. A whole new ball game for young readers!

Invite children to read and respond to several books by Gordon Korman. Talk about a variety of story elements such as characters, settings, and themes. Through this exercise, students may discover pleasing parts for their own stories. Here are some of the observations that even reluctant readers make about Korman's books.

- They are funny, fast-paced, full of adventures, have catchy titles, and are about characters who love to wreak havoc.
- The books' settings include a boarding school, summer camp, music festival, cross-country tour, lodge, and Hollywood movie on location.
- Kids in Korman's books are imaginative, resourceful, witty, intelligent, have some freedom from parental constraints, and solve the problems of the world.
- Gordon Korman often makes fun of adult figures. Some of his bizarre adults include a Grade 5 teacher who conducts a "seminar" all year long, a Ministry of Education inspector who is a closet football addict, and a crazy landlord who goes into business selling hubcaps.

Other Things That Kids Ask about a Lot

Rudy's letter from *I Want to Go Home!* (p. 23): "It's based on the letter I wrote when my parents sent me to camp. (I really did want to go home.)"

"The rock groups from *Who Is Bugs Potter?* were made up before the book. Endomorph was picked, eenie-meenie, out of the dictionary. Dorchester Melon and their *Spitting out the Seeds* album was pure imagination and association of ideas. Nuclear Teacup came straight out of left field."

Korman's main concerns are not the "big" problems like teenage pregnancy, divorce, and drugs, but the "little" things such as personal relationships, having fun, and honesty. To Korman, these things are just as important. His purpose, he says, is to write a good, entertaining story that keeps kid laughing and reading. Judging by the great popularity of his titles, he seems to be succeeding.

3

Author Studies: Ideas, Inspiration, and Information

"Every wonderful author whom I have read has influenced me. I read a truly great book and despair that I will never be able to write that well. Then I try, and I find that the book has become part of me and has taught me something. I've grown, and my writing has stretched because of it."

— Karleen Bradford, in *Writing Stories, Making Pictures*

In recent years, author studies have become an important part of the Language Arts program. As a result, children are more informed about authors and illustrators than ever before. It is not uncommon, for example, to see Grade 1, or even Grade 8, students do an author study (or "arthur" study as many six-year-olds say!) on the popular storyteller Robert Munsch. They can readily list a dozen of his titles and tell what they like about his stories. Some kids can also identify the various illustrators of Robert Munsch's books, as well as the styles and media used in the illustrations (see the feature "Robert Munsch: Picture Book Author" on pages 33–34).

Author studies are valuable at *all grade levels*. In this approach, teachers and students focus on a specific author or illustrator for a certain amount of time — a day, a week, two weeks, or a month. After you read, display, and discuss a collection of books, students do interesting activities related to the work. It would not be fair to limit these activities to five- and six-year-olds — intermediate students revel in these explorations. So do Grade 3 children. Stimulating programs spark enthusiasm and positive thinking at all levels. Creativity follows naturally.

Anyone who has seen the excitement that takes place around authors and illustrators knows the benefits of this approach. Stephanie Harvey puts it best in *Nonfiction Matters*: "Our favourite authors can be our best teachers. We grow to know them through their books, and we learn about writing by reading their work." Quite simply, there is no substitute for learning from a master. Through author studies, children learn to publish like the pros!

Author studies give students insight into writing. They make us aware of the reading/writing connection and inspire kids in their own creativity. Children who are learning to write and illustrate their own stories look up to authors and illustrators as models.

Author studies also develop students' critical sense. Children can learn to notice and use specific writing or illustration styles. The techniques they see motivate them in their own writing and artwork.

Key Reasons for Author Studies

Here are several key reasons for conducting author studies in your classroom.

1. Students can learn a lot about the creative process from authors and illustrators.
2. You can offer them focused exposure to a variety of authors and illustrators.
3. Students can develop an appreciation for authors, illustrators, and their work.
4. You can show the connection between books and real life.
5. You immerse students in reading and stimulate their creativity.
6. Students can glean a purpose for writing, for example, writing a letter to an author or illustrator.
7. You can help children learn new vocabulary which they can apply to their own creative work.

The Value of Author Studies

Author studies can be as simple or as extensive as you wish. Read several books by one author over a period of time and discuss the author's background from the back of the book cover. Or, explore the books in greater depth with activities like the Barbara Reid author study in Chapter 4.

Author studies can be conducted with kids of all ages. Choose writers from a variety of genres, as well as illustrators who work in various media. Students can use the techniques they learn about in their own bookmaking. The object is to introduce them to many creative possibilities.

Author studies can be done as often as you wish. Decide whether you want to focus on a specific author every week, or in two-week blocks, or on a monthly basis. Many classes highlight a different author every month, with exciting follow-up activities. Just think, if you explore a new author each month, you will have exposed your students to ten excellent authors during the school year. That's great!

Author studies can be done as a large group, as a small group or as an independent activity. Author studies are effective with the whole class, particularly when you begin the unit by reading a book aloud to your students. If you teach reading in small groups, you may do a mini-unit with one particular group of students. Students who are in independent reading programs may focus on a selection of titles by one person and extend the learning through related activities.

Four Ways to Choose an Author or Illustrator

Number one: Ask your students who their favorite authors and illustrators are. Find out what books they like by that person and why. Spur them to talk about authors they enjoy now, and from when they were younger. You will learn a lot about your students' reading interests and abilities, and often make surprising discoveries!

When you ask your students who their favorite authors are, anticipate diversity. Use their responses to help determine which authors to focus on. Capitalize on their responses to develop other areas of growth. Don't be discouraged if senior students say Dr. Seuss or Robert Munsch are their favorites, for example. Both of these children's authors are two of the most popular in the world. In this case, look towards literature as a source of humor you and your kids can laugh about together. By reading a funny story aloud and extending those good feelings to related activities, you will help your students develop their own wit as well as class spirit. Remember, picture books are meant for people of all ages. Books by Dr. Seuss and Robert Munsch are fun. Their catchy titles and crazy characters often inspire kids to play with language and emulate their style.

Number two: Choose an author or illustrator whose work *you* admire. Maybe you want to introduce an award-winning writer to your students. It is unnecessary to know all of the authors or their books before an author study. It is exciting to learn with your students. Your goal is to expose your students to excellent writers and illustrators, and contribute to their reading growth.

Number three: Choose a book creator whose work ties in with a particular theme or genre. For example, if you are doing a Northern unit, you may wish to focus on Michael Kusugak, an Inuit storyteller whose stories are based on growing up in the Northwest Territories. Books like *Arctic Tales*, *A Promise Is a Promise*, *Baseball Bats for Christmas*, *Hide and Sneak*, and *Northern Lights: The Soccer Trails* inspire children to write stories which chart important events in their lives.

At some schools, intermediate teachers conduct evening parent-child reading groups, or "literature circles," with great success. Grade 8 teachers, for example, lead enthusiastic groups of kids and parents in lively book discussions. In this thematic approach, a particular book is discussed within the context of related titles. Readers focus on such authors as Monica Hughes, Kit Pearson, Carol Matas, Katherine Paterson, and Jerry Spinelli.

Number four: Finally, you may determine which author or illustrator to study by the guests who come to your school. If you are lucky enough to have an author visit, you will want to familiarize your students with their work ahead of time so that the presentation is meaningful. (See Chapter 5 for more author visit ideas.)

Planning an Author Study

Once you have decided which author or illustrator you are going to study, here's how to get started.

✓ Gather as many of the author's books as you can, either single copies for read-alouds or multiple copies for independent reading.

✓ Display the books so that children see the full covers.

✓ Decide on the scope of your author study. An author may have a series of picture books, as well as assorted non-fiction books, poetry books, books for preschool children, and other fiction books. With younger children, you may want to focus wholly on a picture book series. Older students can explore a wider range of the author's works to get a deeper understanding of the person.

✓ Collect materials about the author, such as videos, audiocassettes, media clippings, photographs, and posters.

✓ Prepare a bulletin board, table, or countertop for posters, pictures, and children's work as the study progresses.

✓ Decide on the amount of time you plan to spend on your author study. You might want to set aside two weeks for a study or spread it over one month.

Getting the Study Under Way

Introduce the author to children either by reading a book aloud or sharing information. Ask students to name any of the author's books they have read and to share what they know about the person, too. Make a list of questions they may have. Children are often curious to learn about the author's childhood, the number of books he or she has made, sources of ideas, book characters, and the artwork.

As with any author study, you and your students will likely spend most of your time reading and responding to the books. Depending on children's grade level and reading ability, you can read the books aloud or have students read them individually, with partners, or in small groups.

You can extend the study through discussion, illustrations, drama, writing, or other creative activities. When you discuss the author's work, consider the author's background, common patterns or themes, characters, plots, and settings; make comparisons to books by other authors, charting similarities and differences; and explore students' personal responses.

With the students' help, make a display of objects related to the author's work. For example, if you are studying storyteller Tololwa Mollel, consider making a display of African artifacts on fabric from Tanzania, his native country. Or, if you are studying a non-fiction writer, such as Pamela Hickman, author of *The Jumbo Book of Nature Science*, children

"To read a writer is for me not merely to get an idea of what he says, but to go off with him, and travel in his company."

— Andre Gide

can make gull-go-rounds hanging from the ceiling, birdfeeders, and nature murals.

This might also be a good time to write to the author (see page 38 for letter writing ideas), arrange for the author to visit, play a tape of the author reading one of his books, or watch a video on the author. As well, you can post students' written responses to the books on a "Meet the Author" bulletin board.

Throughout the study, note your students' responses during discussions, choice of extension activities, level of interest in reading other works by the author/illustrator, and use of the author's or illustrator's style in their personal creativity. Conclude the study by reflecting on what the author's style teaches students as writers, making an author quilt depicting children's favorite books, or planning a special celebration.

FEATURE: Robert Munsch — Picture Book Author

Robert Munsch is one of North America's best-loved storytellers! Ask any group of children how many of them have read at least ten books by Robert Munsch, and watch their eyes light up! Then challenge them to name ten of his more than thirty titles, such as *The Paper Bag Princess, Pigs, Thomas' Snowsuit, I Have to Go!, Mortimer, Something Good, Angela's Airplane, 50 Below Zero, Jonathan Cleaned Up and Then He Heard a Sound, Andrew's Loose Tooth, Stephanie's Ponytail, Alligator Baby,* and *Love You Forever.*

What makes Robert Munsch's books so popular? "They're funny!" kids say. "He writes about things kids can relate to — birthday parties, fire stations, magic markers, and toilet problems!" They also love the pictures. Munsch's stories are contemporary and zany, reflecting "a jaunty belief in the power of children . . . ," says *Horn Book Magazine.*

Surprisingly, Robert Munsch never planned to be an author. He studied to be a Roman Catholic Jesuit priest, then taught nursery school, where he first began storytelling. His worldwide success includes foreign editions of his books in Armenia, Australia, China, Denmark, France, Germany, Greece, Israel, Korea, Latin America, Mexico, The Netherlands, Spain, Sweden, and the U.K. Every year he gets thousands of letters from teachers and students of all grade levels, requesting information and responding to his books.

Here are some ways you might use Munsch's books in your classroom.

- Read several of the author's books with your students, or play a tape of Munsch telling his own stories. Young children may chime in with sound effects. They also love to sing Mortimer's song or the song from *Love You Forever.*
- Robert Munsch is known for his wild and wacky stories. Just for fun, make up a silly story with your class. Begin by offering a story starter aloud. For example: "One day when Jenny and Tony were walking home from school, they saw something very surprising." Invite children to contribute, adding as many outrageous story elements as

they like. Record them and read the results together when you are done.

- Look at the titles of Robert Munsch's books. Discuss the importance of using catchy titles for stories so that your students can apply this understanding to their own work.

- Take a closer look at the pictures. Michael Martchenko has illustrated many, but not all, of Robert Munsch's stories — readers appreciate the humor in his work, especially the details that are not necessarily part of the story. To stimulate interest and curiosity, compare illustrators of the various books. Children will notice the realistic pictures in *Millicent and the Wind* versus the "comic" illustrations of *Pigs*, or the effect of the black-and-white illustrations that appear in the original *Mud Puddle*. Then create a chart of the stories.

Comparing Illustrations in Robert Munsch's Books			
Title	Illustrator	Style	Medium
Pigs	Michael Martchenko	comic	watercolor
Millicent and the Wind	Suzanne Duranceau	realistic	watercolor
Mud Puddle	Sami Suomalainen	between comic & realistic	watercolor
Get Out of Bed!	Alan & Lea Daniel	caricature based on a real family	colored pencil & watercolor
Purple, Green & Yellow	Hélène Desputeaux	comic	watercolor
Ribbon Rescue	Eugenie Fernandes	decorative energetic humorous	gouache and colored pencil
Love You Forever	Sheila McGraw	representational; somewhat Impressionistic	colored pencil and watercolor

- Explain to your students that the story dictates the style of drawing an illustrator uses. Open-ended questions such as "Why do you suppose we see a different illustrator for the same author sometimes?" lead into discussion as children give thoughtful replies, for example:

1. Certain illustration styles suit certain kinds of stories.
2. Illustrators may be working on other projects, so may be unavailable.
3. All books should not look the same.
4. Publishers may want to introduce new illustrators.

All of these activities are fun, but they have a serious purpose, too. It is exciting to respond to literature this way, comparing one book with another. Children see how illustrations should fit the mood of the story, and the publishing process becomes more "real" to them.

Tips for Inspiring Budding Writers

Thought of the Day/Writers' Wisdom: Each day, share a quote or tip from a famous author or illustrator over the intercom. Nothing moves people like first-hand advice and experience! Inspire your students and colleagues to be creative with words of wisdom from popular children's book creators.

Weekly Bulletin Board Features: Make your halls and walls an integral part of your publishing program. Set up a blackboard or bulletin-board display with the heading, "Tips for Young Creators" or "Professional Pointers."

Every week, present a tip from a different author or illustrator to inspire your students. Include photographs if you have them. Your students can research and present the tips. The quotes can come from reference books or Web sites which offer biographies of creators.

> Our featured creator is the author
> Welwyn Wilton Katz
> Her Tips for Young Creators:
> "Read more good books than junk and write every day!"

Rhyme Time: Performer and author Sonja Dunn suggests creating clever rhymes to introduce authors. Here are a few of Dunn's chants:

There's a bunch of books by Munsch
Tasty reading — Crunch! Crunch!
Good for breakfast, good for lunch
Anytime is good for Munsch!
Presenting . . . Robert Munsch

Hands on, thumbs up
Friendship too
Boondoggle bracelets
of orange and blue!
Introducing . . . Camilla Gryski

Janet Lunn —
a frequent winner.
At getting awards
she's no beginner!

She writes about people
and places and books.
She uses time travel
as one of her hooks!
Here's Barbara Greenwood!

Sonja Dunn, who captivates audiences worldwide with her playful poems, reveals: "Often after I visit a school, children send me rhymes they have made up. Kids do a good job of following the patterns." Try it in your class. Read aloud rhymes about different authors, then invite students to create rhymes about their favorite authors. Use them to liven up author activities:

- [ ] as headings for bulletin-board displays;
- [ ] as introductions at author/illustrator visits;
- [ ] as follow-up thank-yous to author visits;
- [ ] and as whole class chants in unison.

"Meet the Author" Bulletin Board: Honor a favorite author with a special bulletin board. Students can design a colorful nameplate, write biographies of the author, draw pictures of their favorite book characters or parts of the author's books, and post all of their creations on the bulletin board. Encourage students to write responses to the author's work too.

Five Fun Author Activities

Author Tree: Make a famous author tree by anchoring a tree branch in a container of sand or Plasticine. Cut out leaf shapes and print the names of famous authors and illustrators on each one. Hang your leaves from the branches with thread. See if your students know what books they made.

Day after Day: Being an author can be difficult. It can be a lot of fun, too. Brainstorm all the ways being a writer can be easy. In what ways is it difficult? Put your students' ideas on a chart with headings like these:

Good Things about Being an Author . . . .

Difficult things about Being an Author . . . .

Let's Compare: After you have read a book by a well-known author or illustrator to your students, encourage them to read another book by the same person. They can then compare the two books with these questions in mind: Where does the story take place. When? What type of story is it? Who are the characters? What style of writing or illustration is there?

Collectables: Publish a class collection about favorite authors and illustrators. Your students can decide which creators they want to feature in the book, and take part in the research. Possible contents:

titles of authors' books	excerpts of writing
awards they have won	photographs
biographies of their lives	drawings
illustrators of their stories	newspaper clippings, advertisements

Children can brainstorm a catchy title for the book and make an interesting cover with pictures from newspapers, magazines, and the Internet, or illustrate it themselves.

Popularity Poll: Find out which authors are most popular in your class. Take a survey by asking each student to name their favorite author or illustrator. Ask children to identify what they have read by that person. Encourage them to explain their choices. This will tell you a lot about the children you are working with, and you'll be able to draw on that knowledge throughout the year. Record their favorite authors on a tally chart similar to the one below to show the results.

Favorite Children's Author/Illustrator Chart	
E.B. White	IIII
Beverly Cleary	HHt III
Martyn Godfrey	HHt
Bernice Thurman Hunter	III
Lucy Maud Montgomery	HHt

After children share who their favorite authors are, interpret the data by asking questions. For example: Which author got the most votes? Which author got the least?

Independent Inquiry

After you have demonstrated several author studies with your class, children may choose any book creator they want to learn more about and do their own inquiry. Following your lead, they can read a particular author's books, learn about the person's work, write a biography, respond to the work, and share tips for children. In short, kids can publish books about their favorite authors and illustrators! Give students practice doing a web outline, like the one on page 96. Or give them an outline similar to the following.

Choose an author or illustrator you would like to know more about. Here are some topics you could include in your project.

☐ biography
☐ bibliography
☐ picture
☐ awards
☐ why you chose this author
☐ your favorite book by this person and why?
☐ style tips

You are welcome to introduce other topics.

Possible Sources of Information

☐ books
☐ observation
☐ the Internet
☐ audiotapes, videotapes
☐ guest speakers

Writing to Authors

Writers in Electronic Residence (WIER)
http://www.wier.yorku.ca/wier/home/

Did you know that kids with computers can become part of a network which connects them to professional writers and illustrators?

In the WIER program, each participating student becomes a member of an intimate writing community linked by an e-mail box information system. Students leave writing assignments (poems, stories, essays) for the writer to access. The writer responds by leaving advice, direction, and editorial comments for students to consider as they explore their writing. The conversations about writing have a powerful effect on young people's feelings about the writing process, and about the particular writer they have been in touch with.

If children want to contact an author or illustrator, direct their letter to the appropriate publisher. Usually, publishers print their address at the beginning of each book, and will pass any note on to the author. Most authors have e-mail too. E-mail enables kids to communicate with authors around the world. In this way, they learn to understand and value other book creators.

Generally, authors like to get mail from their readers. They appreciate feedback on their work, which sometimes leads to more writing ideas. In one unprecedented case, seven-year-old Saoussan Askar wrote a letter to storyteller Robert Munsch. After she told him about her family moving from Beirut, Lebanon, to North America, Munsch co-authored a book with her called *From Far Away*.

Understandably, most authors prefer meaningful letters from individual readers, rather than class sets of generic letters. You can teach students how to write letters that are polite and purposeful. Encourage them to be specific in their questions and comments. They need to know that the recipient is doing a favor if he or she responds. Usually, writers are happy to answer personal letters from thoughtful readers.

Letter-Writing Tips

Children's author Kathy Stinson offers these tips to teachers.

DO encourage kids to write when they have enjoyed a book so much they'd like the author to know, or when a book provokes probing questions they would like to ask the author.

DON'T get kids to write to an author for practice in writing letters. Authors don't need practice writing letters back to students. They need to write more books.

DO make use of the many resources available where interviews with authors and information about them can be found.

DON'T get kids to ask for information from an author which can be obtained in publications. Besides asking authors to take time from their writing to help kids with their projects, it's shortchanging kids on an opportunity to develop research skills.

DO encourage kids to be specific. Doing this reduces the number of generic questions asked about being an "author."

DON'T assign the writing of a "letter to an author" to your whole class. Not all kids are motivated to write; most authors would prefer to see uninspired student-writers being read to, or turned on to books, than being given an assignment which reinforces that writing is drudgery and connects that drudgery to reading books. — *Children's Book News*, Spring 1994

Resources on Book Creators

As more and more children's books have been published, so too, has information about their creators. Today, resources on children's authors and illustrators *abound*, enhancing the school program and reflecting the vitality of children's literature. Now we can enter their world in a way never before possible. More than ever before, we can expose children to a wealth of creativity!

In some places, it is expensive to bring authors in for school visits, so other resources are particularly important. Did you know that you can show your students a video about their favorite author or illustrator? or that students can interact with authors through on-line mentorships? Check with your librarian or media centre about a host of Meet the Author publications and support materials. If not available locally, author information can be obtained from the following organizations, publishers, books, and Web sites.

Organizations in Canada

Organizations play a huge part in creating a rich reading environment. They promote the authors and illustrators who are making a brilliant and distinctive contribution to children's literature, who go above and beyond to connect those books with kids.

The Canadian Children's Book Centre, a national, non-profit organization, provides extensive information on Canadian children's authors and illustrators, gives practical advice to budding writers and illustrators, and produces publications full of programming ideas, and more. Contact any one of the regional offices or the national office at

35 Spadina Road, Toronto, ON M5R 2S9
Phone: (416) 975-0010; fax: (416) 975-1839; e-mail: ccbc@sympatico.ca;
Web site: http://www3.sympatico.ca/ccbc

Communication Jeunesse offers a gold mine of information if you teach French, or are interested in French-Canadian authors and illustrators. You can reach Communication Jeunesse at

5307 boul. St-Laurent, Montréal, PQ H2T 1S5
Phone: (514) 273-8167; fax: (514) 271-6812;
Web site: http://pages.infinit.net/livrocj

CANSCAIP (The Canadian Society of Children's Authors, Illustrators and Performers) is a group of professionals in the field of children's culture with members from all parts of Canada. The organization provides a listing of members available for workshops in children's literature, creative writing, drawing, puppetry, clowning, mime, storytelling, and drama; plus exhibits, newsletters, publications, and more. For more information, contact CANSCAIP at

35 Spadina Road, Toronto, ON M5R 2S9
Phone: (416) 515-1559; fax: (416) 515-7022;
Web site: http://www. interlog.com/~canscaip

Read Up on It! is the National Library's Web site where you can find annotated lists of books published in Canada on various themes and award-winning titles; photographs, biographies, and bibliographies of Canadian authors and illustrators; and interactive games for children and young adults. Contact *Read Up on It!* at

National Library of Canada,
395 Wellington Street, Ottawa ON K1A 0N4
Phone: (613) 995-7969; fax: (613) 991-9871;
e-mail: publications@nic-bnc.ca; Web site: www.nlc-bnc.ca/ruoi/

Organizations outside Canada

The Children's Book Council is a non-profit trade organization that has been dedicated to encouraging literacy and the enjoyment of children's books since 1945. It offers programming pertinent to all professionals working with children's books, including teachers and librarians, as well as parents. It also sponsors educational programs with the American Library Association and the International Reading Association. Contact the Children's Book Council at

568 Broadway, Suite 404, New York, NY 10012
Phone: (212) 966-1990; fax: (212) 966-2073;
Web site: http://www.cbcbooks.org

Children's Book Foundation is a non-profit organization in the United Kingdom. Celebrating Children's Book Week in schools, libraries, bookstores, and homes across the U.K. is a major part of its work. Contact Children's Book Foundation at

45 East Hill, London SW18 2QZ
Phone: 10-870-9055

Publishers

Many publishers produce free author and illustrator profiles to help publicize their books. You can contact them by phone or e-mail. Better yet, encourage your students to write letters to publishers requesting information. Publishers print their addresses at the front of books.

If your author is published by a large company, contact the publicity manager. He or she organizes all aspects of promotion, such as producing special publicity material. If you tell the publicity manager that you are studying one of that company's authors, you may receive photos, bibliographies, newspaper clippings, teacher's guides, bookmarks, or posters. Publishers can also advise you on the availability of their authors or illustrators to visit your school in person.

Book clubs

Creating an Author File

You may find it helpful to set up a binder or a folder to collect author profiles. They serve as background for your students' individual reading as well as class author studies.

Often, book clubs feature reader-friendly author/illustrator profiles. Letters from authors offer childhood recollections and wonderful advice for children who like to write. Occasionally book clubs hold Win-an-Author contests — your chance to win a popular author for a day in your classroom! Book clubs introduce you to some of the best children's authors and illustrators.

Books

Books are a great source of information about many children's writers and illustrators. Use them to gain insight into their working practices, influences, and aspirations. Begin with the following:

- *Behind the Story: The People Who Create Our Best Children's Books . . . and How They Do It!*, edited by Barbara Greenwood
- *The CANSCAIP Companion: A Biographical Record of Canadian Children's Authors, Illustrators and Performers*, 2d ed., edited by Barbara Greenwood
- *Meet the Authors and Illustrators: 60 Creators of Favorite Children's Books Talk about Their Work*, by Deborah Kovacs and James Preller
- *Meet the Authors and Illustrators: Volume 2*, by Deborah Kovacs and James Preller
- *Meet Canadian Authors and Illustrators: 50 Creators of Children's Books*, by Allison Gertridge
- *Presenting Children's Authors, Illustrators and Performers*, edited by Barbara Greenwood
- *The Storymakers: Illustrating Children's Books, Biographies of 72 Artists & Illustrators*, by The Canadian Children's Book Centre

The Internet

Many Web sites are designed to help you plan author studies and publishing programs. The Internet serves as a huge information and reference source. You can use it to correspond with authors, illustrators, and publishers; plan author visits; get tips from professionals; and celebrate special events such as Children's Book Week. Kids can access information and help from authors and illustrators.

The Internet also opens doors to many authentic experiences. A child writing a story can submit a piece of work to a professional author via e-mail and receive feedback on it through the Internet. Students are highly motivated to write stories when provided with real opportunities to interact with authors. When encouraged by published authors, they want to improve their writing. The Web sites listed here include authors' personal Web sites as well as those maintained by fans, scholars, and readers.

- *Children's Literature Web Guide* at
  http://www.acs.ucalgary.ca/~dkbrown/authors.html
- *Invite an Author* at http://www.snowcrest.net/kidpower/authors.html
- *The Writers' Union of Canada* at http://www.swifty.com/twuc
- *Best Books for Kids* at http://www.bestkidsbooks.com

Go Surfing

You and your students can check out the Web sites of popular authors
and illustrators! See favorite characters, watch for new books, and send
e-mail.

Eric Carle
www.eric-carle.com

Jim Aylesworth
www.ayles.com

Dav Pilkey
www.pilkey.com

Audrey Wood
www.audreywood.com

Tedd Arnold
www.geocities.com/athens
/delphi/9096

Roald Dahl
http://www.nd.edu/~khoward1/
dahl/

Seymour Simon
http://www.pipeline.com/
~simonsi/

Avi
www.avi-writer.com

Debbie Dadey & Marcia Thornton
Jones
www.baileykids.com

Jean Craighead George
http://jeancraigheadgeorge.com

Marc Brown
www.marcbrown.com

Katherine Paterson
http://www.terabithia.com

Lucy Maud Mongomery
http://www.upei.ca/~Immi/core.
html

Robert Munsch
www.robertmunsch.com

Jan Brett
www.janbrett.com

Stan and Jan Berenstain
www.berenstainbears.com

Hans Wilhelm
www.hanswilhelm.com

Werner Zimmermann
www.sentex.net/~zimmy/

Madeline L'Engle
http://www.geocities.com/Athens
/Acropolis/8838/

Jerry Spinelli
http://www.car.lib.md.us/authco/
spinelli-j.htm

Cynthia Rylant
www.rylant.com

Jahnna N. Malcolm
www.jewelkingdom.com

Karen Hesse
www.riverdale.k12.or.us/~cmaxwel
/hesse.htm

Phoebe Gilman
www.phoebegilman.com

Jack London
http://sunsite.berkeley.edu/
London/

Jon Scieszka and Lane Smith
http://www.chucklebait.com

Author videos

Invite your favorite authors into your classroom and watch their stories come to life!

Meet the Author Live Action Videos is an excellent series in which authors and illustrators ruminate on childhood adventures, inspiration, work habits, family, and career. Each program presents authors and illustrators at work discussing various aspects of their craft. Many school libraries have copies. If not, you may borrow them from your media centre or public library.

Some titles in the series:

*Marie-Louise Gay**   *Robert Munsch**
Martyn Godfrey   *Barbara Reid**
Camilla Gryski   *David Suzuki*
Marilyn Halvorson   *C. J. Taylor**
Gordon Korman   *Gilles Tibo**
Jean Little   *Ian Wallace*
Kevin Major   *Eric Wilson*
*Lucy Maud Montgomery**   *Paul Yee*

*Videos available in both English and French

The following organizations carry titles in this series:

School Services of Canada
176 Albany Ave.
Toronto, ON
M5R 3C6
(416) 410-7465

The Canadian Children's Book
Centre
35 Spadina Rd.
Toronto, ON
M5R 2S9
(416) 975-0010

Academic Minds Inc.
11 Cosmo Rd.
Toronto, ON
M8X 1Z3
(416) 236-0770

Delta Education
Box 915
Hudson, NH
03051
(603) 598-7170

Note: Usually, author videotapes are available for purchase only. Most of the tapes are in VHS format and are approximately twenty minutes long.

Today, more than ever before, children have opportunities to find out about the authors whose books they enjoy and admire. Not only can they become familiar with authors' lives and sources of inspiration, they can build on that knowledge to spark their own creativity. What's true for young adult fiction writer Monica Hughes can be true for them. In *Writing Stories, Making Pictures*, Hughes wrote of the authors she knew and admired: "These authors became my teachers. Through them, I learned to write — I am still learning to write." What could be better models for young authors than the professional writers whose books excite them?

4

A Model Author Study:
Barbara Reid

"Have you seen calves?
Have you seen birds?
It's a Plasticine party.
She's also gifted with words!
Introducing . . . Barbara Reid."

— Sonja Dunn

Since *The New Baby Calf* was first published in 1984, Barbara Reid has become one of the best-known children's illustrators. She is famous for her Plasticine art, in which she creates textured pictures from the oil-based modeling clay. Teachers and students are spellbound by her work. Not only has she won top honors for her books, but she has revolutionized the use of Plasticine in schools.

Every teacher I know has either done an author study on Barbara Reid — or wants to. That is why I have chosen this gifted author and illustrator as the subject of a detailed author study. In this chapter you and your students will "meet Barbara Reid" and find answers to many of the questions children ask about her. You will gain suggestions for studying Reid's distinct style and, of course, ways to make Plasticine masterpieces with your students. Use the chapter as a model to study other excellent authors and illustrators.

Favorite Barbara Reid Books

The New Baby Calf, by Edith Newlin Chase. Illustrations by
    Barbara Reid
Have You Seen Birds?, by Joanne Oppenheim. Illustrations by
    Barbara Reid
Sing a Song of Mother Goose, compiled by Barbara Reid
Effie, by Beverly Allinson. Illustrations by Barbara Reid
The *Zoe* series: *Zoe's Windy Day*, *Zoe's Rainy Day*, *Zoe's Sunny Day*, and
    Zoe's Snowy Day, by Barbara Reid. Illustrations by the author
Two by Two, by Barbara Reid. Illustrations by the author
Gifts, by Jo Ellen Bogart. Illustrations by Barbara Reid
The Party, by Barbara Reid. Illustrations by the author
Fun with Modeling Clay, by Barbara Reid. Illustrations by the author
First Look series: *Caterpillar to Butterfly*, *Acorn to Oak Tree*, *Tadpole to Frog*,
    Seed to Flower, by Barbara Reid. Illustrations by the author

---

Getting Organized for Your Author Study

✓ Gather as many of Barbara Reid's books as you can. Try to get several copies of each book for read-alouds and independent reading.

✓ Display the books on a table, blackboard ledge, bookshelf, or countertop that allows children to see full covers.

✓ Check for author profiles in books, as well as in videos such as the *Meet the Author* feature.

✓ Promote your author study on classroom walls. Try making a Plasticine sign with Barbara Reid's name on it for your bulletin-board display. You might also show Sonja Dunn's rhyme (see first sidebar of chapter) to introduce the author!

✓ Decide on how long you want to spend studying Barbara Reid and her books. Allow two to four weeks so that you can touch on different aspects of her work.

✓ Create response journals for children: to make a journal, stack together several sheets and staple at the top left-hand corner. After you finish reading each Barbara Reid book, have children respond to it in their journals.

Introducing the Author

Introduce Barbara Reid by reading one of her books aloud and focusing on the Plasticine pictures. Ask children to share what they know about Barbara Reid and to name any of her books they have already read. Make a list of questions that children have about the book creator and her work, and see if these questions can be answered during the unit. This might be a good time to watch a video on Barbara Reid. After you read more of her books, you can explore her unique style in greater depth.

An award-winning book creator

Barbara Reid was born on November 16, 1957, and grew up in Toronto, Ontario. After graduating from high school, she attended the Ontario College of Art. She has always worked as a freelance illustrator. In 1984 she illustrated *The New Baby Calf*, and has since written and/or illustrated many books. Barbara Reid has won more than twenty awards, including the coveted international prize, the Ezra Jack Keats Award. Reid lives in Toronto with her husband and their two daughters.

Barbara Reid, the Illustrator: As far back as she can remember, Barbara Reid loved to read and draw. Early in her life she remembers making all sorts of creatures and contraptions. "When I was little my mom would give me some modeling clay, and I'd play happily all day. I'd make buildings, people, animals, even whole villages."

She began illustrating books before she began writing them. Her pictures are made with Plasticine that is shaped and pressed onto illustration board. Sometimes, she uses acrylic glaze or paint for shiny effects. Each of her richly textured illustrations conveys movement and relationships, through line and depth of color.

Barbara Reid, the Storyteller: Reid has written, as well as illustrated, several of her own books. She considers herself a storyteller, telling stories through art and words.

She often takes writing classes which let her experiment with new techniques and also get feedback from other group members. She stresses that it "takes a lot of work" to create children's books. Whether she's writing about a family reunion or Noah's Ark, she captures the readers' attention with warmth, freshness of style, and a ready wit.

Plasticine Picture Books from Start to Finish

Barbara Reid explains how she makes her books: "Making a picture book takes a long time and many people to help create it. I spend a few weeks thinking about the story and collect research that I may need from the library. Then I plan all the pictures with pencil and paper. These drawings are called roughs.

"Usually I draw the main characters many times to get used to them and understand how they look moving around. In *Two by Two* I decided early on to give Noah a very long beard — he was very old and wise. I like Turkish costumes for the people — they fit the time and place.

"Next is a storyboard. I draw each spread of the book in a small rough format and indicate type. It gives me an overall plan and helps pace the book and prevent repetition. Deciding what words go where and what size each illustration will be takes a long time with many changes.

"I buy Plasticine in many different colors. To get even more, I mix colors. For example, kneading white and red Plasticine makes pink. The pictures are made on illustration board or stiff cardboard. First, I spread a thin background layer with my thumbs. This provides a sticky surface to add on smaller details and textures. I make shapes in my fingers and press them on, building up the layers. Round pancake shapes can be pebbles on a beach or somebody's fat cheeks. Rolling out a long snake shape can make hair, a kite string, or smoke rising from a chimney.

"I use some tools: a knife to cut shapes like fence posts and doors; a comb to press a grassy or furry texture into the Plasticine; a sharp pencil to poke whisker lines or nostrils or nail holes with. I use my imagination to think up textures I want and I look around the house for tools to help me. Most of my Plasticine pictures are two times larger than the finished book. That way I can get more detail in.

"Each page in a book takes up to three days to make in Plasticine. A large picture, like the owl in *Have You Seen Birds?*, takes about three days. When all the pictures are finished, we photograph the work. My husband, Ian Crysler, is a professional photographer. He photographs my work. Each piece is carefully lit so that it looks three-dimensional in the book. The whole process — from the writer's idea to a finished book — can take a year or more. The nice part is that a good book lasts forever; it's always a thrill for me to open up a book that I helped to make."

Five questions kids ask about Barbara Reid

1. *Does Barbara Reid do all her pictures in Plasticine?*

   Actually, no. She illustrates books such as *How to Make Pop-ups, Have Fun with Magnifying*, and *Just Desserts* using other media, but we know her best for her Plasticine art.

2. *How did Barbara Reid get the idea to do pictures in Plasticine?*

   In 1979, when Reid was a student at art college, a school project required that she re-create a famous painting in another medium. Choosing Botticelli's The Birth of Venus, she decided to use tissue paper. But the night before the deadline, her project wasn't working. So she tried Plasticine! Her assignment was a success, paving the way for many prize-winning illustrations.

3. *What does she do with all her Plasticine pictures?*

   Once the book is done, Barbara Reid frames her pictures and displays them for others to see. People like to buy her original Plasticine art to hang in their homes and offices.

4. *How does she get the Plasticine so soft?*

   Reid uses only small portions at a time. She says "hand heat" works best.

5. *Where does she get all the Plasticine?*

   Like all artists, Barbara Reid buys her own materials. Plasticine is usually available in arts and crafts stores, office supply stores, and toy stores.

Exploring Barbara Reid's Books

Read as many of Barbara Reid's books as you can, and take time to study the illustrations. She includes a lot of detail in her artwork to produce different effects in various ways. The longer you look at her pictures, the more details you see. Ask children which ones they notice (responses will vary depending on children's ages and visual literacy). Some of these details might be, as follows:

Teaching Activities for *Two by Two*

Two by Two was originally called Noah's Ark. Ask your students why they think the title was changed. Why is it important to have catchy titles for books? Brainstorm other title possibilities for the story of Noah's Ark.

Two by Two is based on the song "Who Built the Ark?" (words and music appear at the end of the book). Sing this song with your class. List other books that come from popular songs. Brainstorm what other songs might make good book possibilities.

Show children the endpapers which tie in with the Noah's Ark theme. At the front is a rainstorm pattern in Plasticine and at the back — a rainbow! Once children are familiar with endpapers they may wish to create them in their own books.

☐ use of color in a variety of ways. For example, on the cover of *Two by Two*, dark letters show up well on a light background (white clouds). Explain that this is contrast. Blending together different colors adds depth and richness.

☐ creation of texture, or representation of surface, by building up layers of Plasticine. For example, in *Have You Seen Birds?*, this technique gives the hunting owl its feathery appearance. Reid also uses tools to give objects such as bears and curtains a three-dimensional look.

Help children find examples of the different techniques Reid uses. Encourage them to experiment with these techniques in their own artwork.

If you are working with children in older grades, discuss common themes that the students see in Barbara Reid's work. Many of Reid's books deal with nature, time, change, relationships, and growing up. *The New Baby Calf* is told with subtle charm as it depicts the bond between a calf and its mother. *Gifts* bridges the generations between a grandmother and a granddaughter. *Have You Seen Birds?* offers lively verse descriptions of birds. Through each page runs the warmth of their relationships and appreciation of life's joys. To help children reflect on the themes, create a chart with the headings Title and Theme. Fill in the chart as you discuss each book.

If you are working with children in Kindergarten or early primary grades, or children learning a second language, wordless picture books, such as Barbara Reid's two series, are a useful literary device. Share titles such as *Zoe's Sunny Day*, *Zoe's Rainy Day*, *Zoe's Windy Day*, *Zoe's Snowy Day*, *Caterpillar to Butterfly*, *Acorn to Oak Tree*, *Tadpole to Frog*, and *Seed to Flower*. Ask your children to tell the stories orally, write narratives, give readings of their stories, or create their own wordless picture book to show classmates.

Taking a Closer Look

Clever Details: Barbara Reid's work is full of details that reward children's close attention. Sometimes these details subtly depict an additional subtext imagined by the illustrator, working independently of the author. For example, spring is in the air when we meet the new baby calf in Reid's first book. As we follow the calf's growth, spring turns to fall in the background illustrations — a delightful added dimension to the poem. Can children identify additional subtexts in Reid's other books?

Love of Animals: Reid shares with readers her love of animals and nature. While spending time at her family cottage, she observes wildflowers, insects, and birds, and stores these images for future reference. Guide the children in examining the abundance of wildflowers in *The New Baby Calf*, the realism of the birds' habitats in *Have You Seen Birds?*, the playfulness of animals in *Effie*, and the diversity of creatures in *Two by Two*.

Sense of Humor: Barbara Reid's great sense of humor comes through in her art and stories. *The Party* captures all the fuss and fun of a family get-together — the games, the food, the people — in rhythmic text and comical illustrations. Early on, we are treated to a large, close-up view of Aunt Joan wearing a bright yellow dress and big blue earrings. Her ruby red lips are puckered to greet guests as they arrive at the party. The book is fun to look at, fun to read, and fun to share! Children will enjoy looking for other examples of humor in Reid's work.

Playfulness: Reid also delivers a high-spirited playfulness in *Effie*. Effie is a tiny ant with a voice like thunder. Whenever she speaks, all the insects run to escape from the noise! This book makes for a fun read-aloud. In it you'll find a variety of bugs, each with footwear to match their characters. Have the class look for Effie wearing sensible black Oxfords, a grasshopper wearing red high-top running shoes, a butterfly in ballet slippers, and a caterpillar with yellow thongs on all its little legs. "The bugs began from real insects but evolved into more colorful, imaginary creatures to suit the story," Reid explains. After reading the book, ask children what each character's shoes tell us about their personality.

A Family Connection: Besides being an award-winning author and illustrator, Barbara Reid is a mother of two daughters, Zoe and Tara. Both children appear in her work. The *Zoe* series, for example, features Zoe as a baby during all the seasons of the year. We meet smiling Tara on the last page of *Gifts*. Zoe and Tara are the two girls in *The Party*. Encourage children to include familiar faces and places in their own work.

Different Perspectives: Barbara Reid is a master at using different perspectives in her books, including close-ups of characters, bird's eye views, and ant's eye views. She also skilfully incorporates different kinds of illustrations, such as two-page spreads and pages with two or three small pictures. Invite children to find examples of each type of illustration. Discuss why she may have chosen this type of picture in each case. Explain that Barbara Reid makes a storyboard, or series of small, rough sketches, to plan how a book will look. Suggest that children make storyboards for their books too.

Effie, as sketched by Barbara Reid

Stepping back to graph

After you have finished reading all of Barbara Reid's books, invite children to vote on which they like best and to explain their choices. Make a graph with the heading "What Is Your Favorite Barbara Reid Book?" List the book titles along the bottom of the graph. Children can print their names on self-sticking paper and place the Post-its above their favorite titles. After you interpret the data together, post the chart on your Barbara Reid bulletin board.

Playing with Plasticine

Making Pictures like a Pro

To make Plasticine pictures, follow these three steps from award winner Barbara Reid.

1. Spread a background on a piece of cardboard. Don't worry if it's not perfectly smooth!
2. Make a shape by hand and press it down on the background.
3. Add texture by impressing objects gently into the surface.

Barbara Reid's art inspires children everywhere to make Plasticine pictures of their own. All they need are a few lumps of Plasticine, some household "tools," and a little imagination. First, allow kids time for free play with Plasticine. Start small by building basic shapes such as balls, eggs, pancakes, drops, snakes, and spaghetti strips.

To make Plasticine pictures in your classroom, adopt these practical pointers:

✓ Send a note to parents, asking for "tool bags" filled with toothpicks, plastic-serrated knives, forks, toothbrushes, and sharp pencils.

✓ Cut stiff cardboard into 8.5 in. x 10 in. or 5 in. x 7 in. sheets, depending on picture size. Use the rough side of the cardboard to help the Plasticine stick.

✓ Roll lumps of Plasticine into small balls for each student.

✓ Store Plasticine in yogurt containers or ziplock bags, or use one egg carton per child to organize colors. Children can mix new colors, too.

✓ Protect desks with plastic sheets or linoleum floor mats.

✓ Cover the cardboard with a thin background layer of Plasticine and thin layers for other details.

✓ Since Plasticine is oil-based and won't wash easily, for cleanup, simply rub your hands with dry paper towel.

Plasticine activity suggestions

Funny Faces: Barbara Reid is an expert at making faces in Plasticine. Take a close look at some of the characters' faces in her books. Children can lay down a background in Plasticine and then make faces of their own.

Animals, Animals, Animals: Barbara Reid likes creating animals in Plasticine. Children can choose their favorite animal and make a Plasticine picture. Then they can create a background to show where this animal lives and share their work.

Rhyme Time: After you read *Sing a Song of Mother Goose*, have children choose a Mother Goose rhyme, write it on good paper, and illustrate it in Plasticine. Encourage them to place a funny detail or hidden joke in their pictures.

Self-portraits: Students can create their self-portraits in Plasticine, then check with their friends for likeness.

Fantasy World: Have children sketch a fantasy creature such as a dragon, unicorn, or monster, then create their character in Plasticine. They may attach explanatory notes about the creature's appearance and personality, or write a story and display their work.

It's All in the Name: Barbara Reid makes Plasticine letters for the titles of most of her books. Children can create a colorful Plasticine sign for your Barbara Reid bulletin board or display table.

Keeping Parents Informed

Remember, parents enjoy hearing about your class activities. Some of them may wish to extend the learning at home. You can incorporate a note much like the following into your monthly newsletter or send it on its own:

Dear Parents:

This month we are studying author/illustrator Barbara Reid. Her award-winning Plasticine art is a favorite with children around the world. Titles include <u>Two by Two</u>, <u>Effie</u>, <u>Have You Seen Birds?</u>, <u>Sing a Song of Mother Goose</u>, <u>The New Baby Calf</u>, <u>Gifts</u>, and <u>The Party</u>.

After we have read and discussed many of Barbara Reid's books, we will be making Plasticine pictures of our own. Please send an egg carton and a few "tools" from home, such as tooth-picks, plastic serrated knives, forks, toothbrushes, and sharp pencils, in a plastic bag labeled with your child's name.

You may wish to visit the public library or bookstore to share Barbara Reid's books at home.

Happy reading!
(Your child's teacher)

P.S. Here's a great gift idea: Barbara Reid's how-to book <u>Fun with Modeling Clay</u> and some modeling clay. These are suitable to your child's age, relatively inexpensive, and available locally.

Bringing the Study to Completion

Now that you've spent time exploring Barbara Reid's books with your class, you're ready to finish the unit. Here are some possible activities.

- Ask students to draw conclusions about why they think so many people enjoy Barbara Reid's books.
- Summarize various techniques Reid uses that children can consider adopting for their own projects.

- Plan a Barbara Reid day to celebrate the end of the study.

  Let children make invitations for family members.

  Ask children to share what they've learned about Barbara Reid.

  Display children's writing, artwork, and graphs created during the study.

  Invite children to read aloud favorite Barbara Reid books.

  Ask family members which books they like best, and why.

To some degree, the response of your students will determine the extent to which you study a particular author. When it comes to Barbara Reid, students are often bursting with questions about her work. This chapter offers many fun-filled activities for exploring her books. Plan your time accordingly to suit your individual classroom needs.

5

Hosting a Successful Author/Illustrator Visit

Remember the magic the last time an author visited your school? how inspired the children were and how the author's books leaped off the shelves in the following weeks? the outpouring of art and stories that took place after an illustrator came to your classroom? Anyone who has seen the excitement when an author comes to visit knows that the rewards are great.

An author or illustrator visit is a special event. The presentations provide an excellent chance to learn more about the process of writing and illustrating stories. Kids realize that there are real people behind books and that they, too, can follow their aspirations. For some students, meeting an author is a thrill of a lifetime that they will remember for many years.

Meeting a real author or illustrator can be an intimate, empowering experience for students and teachers. But successful author visits don't happen by magic: the good ones are well planned. Try to involve children as much as possible in the event. It is important to meet the needs of your students as well as your guest. Keeping it manageable is the secret of success. And planning is the key!

Deciding Who to Invite

Decide who you want to invite to your school. Naturally, some people present better than others. Take some time to make an informed choice of who you want to ask. Which books are most popular with the students? What themes will you be working on? Which authors or illustrators have you heard make good presentations?

To find out who is available to do what kind of workshops, contact the organizations identified on pages 39–40. Make a list of the people you'd like to visit your school. You can also consult school and public librarians and publishers for advice. Publishers can help you make contact with their authors. If a well-known author is unavailable, consider choosing a new writer. Often, a newer author is a more likely candidate for a visit.

If you are contacting an author or illustrator directly, discuss these issues:

- ❏ number of presentations to be made;
- ❏ fee for the visit;
- ❏ audience size the author prefers;
- ❏ kind of space he or she likes to speak in;
- ❏ appropriate grade levels;
- ❏ length of the presentation;
- ❏ equipment needed;
- ❏ preferred room arrangement.

Make sure that the author's requirements match your needs and objectives.

Representing the audience's interests

Presentations vary, depending on the person and the grade levels of children in the audience. Generally, book creators discuss their work, describe the publishing process using original materials, read from their books, and give tips to budding writers and illustrators. Build in time for students to ask questions. Talking to professionals can add perspective for those who are particularly interested in writing or illustration. Remember: During presentations every question asked is an indication of interest. Welcome it!

Establishing the Details of the Visit

Be clear about the presentation and the audience make-up. Then inform your colleagues so they can prepare for the event. Doing this will ensure a rewarding experience for all.

Choosing the date

Timing is important for a successful author visit. Effective presentations take place when students have time to get ready for the occasion. A good general rule is to plan three to six months ahead. Avoid scheduling a visit at the end of a term, or on a day when another event is planned. Also, consider how you want to follow up the event.

Location, location, location!

The library is the best setting for an author visit. Most libraries provide a cozy, intimate feeling where everyone is surrounded by books. Students can sit on the floor or at tables or in rows of chairs, depending on the nature of the presentation. Lighting and sound are also important factors. A well-lit room free from disruptive noise and echoes is essential. Again, consult with the presenter so you can set up in advance.

Budget considerations

A fee is always due to the author or illustrator. Fees should be paid on or before the day of the visit. Various sources of support (government or school board) may be available to help you pay for the event. Usually, funds come from the school rather than the district.

Touring authors are often booked for large schools. If you teach in a small, outlying school where an author visit is beyond your budget, consider bring students from another school to your location, and sharing the expense. Or, perhaps your school board and the public library can jointly fund the visit to reduce your cost. The public library could pay for the meals, accommodation, and local transportation while your school pays the cost of the workshop. This arrangement is one way for smaller schools to have equal access to author visits.

Where no outside funding is available, enterprising parent associations and local businesses will often raise money to pay for an author visit. Such support is essential to help ensure a high level of literature-based focus in *all* schools at *all* grade levels.

Confirm details in writing

After you have set a date for the visit, you and your guest should each follow up with a confirmation letter. Send your guest directions to your school, which your students can help to write and show on a map; a schedule of the day (including times and grades of each presentation); parking and unloading information; and lunch plans, if applicable.

The Big Day and Beyond

Here are some helpful tips to keep in mind as you prepare for an author visit.

✓ Check your camera, VCR, and other equipment you intend to use to be sure everything works.
✓ Make sure there are copies of the guest's books in your library.

- ✓ Have children read at least one book by the author or illustrator before the visit.
- ✓ Share biographical information about the person with your students.
- ✓ Organize displays on the works of the visiting author or illustrator, perhaps involving students.

Publicizing the presentation

- ✓ In the school newsletter, inform parents of the visit as it relates to your program.
- ✓ You might have children write invitation letters to parents, school officials, and other interested parties.
- ✓ Inform newspapers and radio and TV stations that a special event is happening at your school. Invite the media to attend and interview your guest afterwards.
- ✓ Invite children to make banners and posters to advertise the event. Place banners in high traffic areas such as the front hall and library to welcome your visitor to the school.
- ✓ Remind students and staff members of the visit.
- ✓ On the big day, welcome your guest over the P.A. system. Involve children in writing the welcome and introduction.

Hired help

Everything will be easier — and more meaningful — if you have help. Children can assist with greetings and introductions as well as with thank-yous and cleanup. Again, involve children in the event wherever possible. This is excellent experience for them!

Helpers can make the difference between a frantic versus a smooth-running day. Before your guest arrives, students can help set up the room. "Porters" can greet the author at the door and help unload materials from the car. While you get the coffee, greeters can show your guest the washroom; while you monitor students entering the room, greeters can make sure there are enough chairs for the adults.

Suggestions for working with student helpers
- Discuss beforehand in detail how to share the responsibilities.
- Be specific in what you will need help with.
- Assign specific jobs to *someone*, to avoid confusion about who is doing what.

   On the day of the visit, students can help you in several ways:
   to set up the room;
   to meet the guest upon arrival and help him/her with their belongings;

to orient the guest to the building, for example, noting where washroom facilities and the coat check are;
to introduce the guest;
to thank the guest;
to help the guest carry out belongings; and
to help clean up.

Setting the stage for manners

Naturally, you'd like everyone to be their best when you have a visitor
in your school. In most cases, they are. Special events can bring out the
worst in some children, though. Try not to ruin the presentation by
scolding. Talk about the event beforehand. Tell your students what to
expect. Let them know whether to ask questions during or after the presentation, and if autographing is encouraged. (Check with your guest
on this.)

A good practice is to develop ahead of time a list of questions that
would be appropriate for children to ask the author or illustrator.
Children may want to learn about their guest's childhood, number of
books written, characters created, writing style, source of ideas, and tips
for their own work. Then, you might want to discuss *inappropriate* questions, such as "How much money do you earn?" or "Are you famous?"
Encourage your students to pose questions that touch on different aspects of the author's *work*.

Although etiquette may seem to be a matter of common sense to most
teachers, some people forget that they are important role models to
their students. Imagine an author giving a presentation to sixty students
while two teachers stand at the back talking to each other, or mark
books! Although such behavior is not necessarily meant as disrespect for
the guest, the results can still be negative. Show by personal example
how to be a good audience. Children are not the only ones who benefit
from author visits. These presentations are excellent professional development. You can take notes during the talk and look for ways to follow
up later.

An author visit should be a special occasion for everyone. Remember
that when authors visit schools, they are doing an important job. Each
visitor brings specialized information, a professional background, and
various materials which will help make the presentation effective. For
these reasons, hosts should make sure that their guests are treated with
respect and attention.

Introducing a special guest

Consider making a straightforward introduction yourself. Go through
information you have and pick out relevant parts to tell the audience;
then, compose your thoughts, concentrating on the focus of the presentation and how it will benefit your students. Be brief! Assuming that
you've checked with your speaker ahead of time, remind the audience

what to expect about asking questions, obtaining autographs, and so on, and welcome the guest to your school.

Better yet, use this opportunity to help children practise public speaking and participate more fully in the event. If you are screening candidates to introduce an author or illustrator, look for a creative student who may consider making up a rhyme (like those on page 35) or dressing up as a book character. When you select students to introduce and thank special guests, you give them a strong sense of responsibility and excellent experience facing an audience! Just be sure to arrange this with the children ahead of time, so that they can plan what to say.

With your class, you might explore what makes a good introduction. Your list of considerations should include the following:

- ❏ use of most relevant background information;
- ❏ accuracy of information;
- ❏ name the visitor prefers to go by;
- ❏ main focus of the presentation and how it will benefit the students;
- ❏ any special directions, e.g., when to ask questions;
- ❏ warmth of welcome.

If you're unaccustomed to public speaking or you wish to help students improve their speaking efforts, these suggestions might help:

- Most people should speak a bit louder than normal.
- Avoid reading notes. Trust yourself.
- Spend fix or six seconds looking at various individuals in the audience. Shorter times can make you seem like "a scared rabbit."

Bringing the visit to a close

You have all had a great time with the author, and now you need to bring closure to the visit. Again, take this opportunity to involve your students. Let children share what they've learned about writing or illustrating, or ask one student, chosen ahead of time, to thank the visitor for coming. In addition, you may wish to express appreciation and embrace your guest's philosophy: "In the next few months, we will continue to practise our writing skills as we strive to become better writers . . . Thanks again for coming to our school."

You will want everyone to feel that the author visit was successful. Here are some ways of reinforcing this perception.

- ✓ Share positive comments with your staff and students over the P.A. system.
- ✓ Send a thank-you note to your guest. Let a child sign off or draw on the note that you write.
- ✓ Add photos, pictures, and comments from students and teachers to your bulletin-board display.

✓ Ask your students to write about the event and incorporate highlights in your newsletter.

✓ Follow up with related activities.

Then, begin planning who you would like to invite next time!

FEATURE: Children's Book Week

Celebrate children's literature for a designated week at your school. Here are some ideas for doing so.

- Study an author a day, have an author birthday party, or arrange for an author visit.
- Dress up as children's book characters.
- Have a parade, put on plays, visit the library.
- Present a poetry festival.
- Ask each child to bring in and read a favorite poem, or create one.
- Establish amnesty for overdue library books. Best excuse wins a prize!
- Provide related arts and crafts projects.
- Let kids make their own bookmarks, banners, quilts, posters — or books.
- Start a promotion and publicity course.
- Encourage kids to write ads to promote Book Week on the intercom, in the school newsletter, or on radio/TV stations.
- Have a book sharing.
- Organize read-alouds, discussions, book swaps, book raffles, sleep-over read-a-thons, and story hours.
- Agree to a week of no TV.
- Sign a pledge, wear a button, carry a sign: *During Book Week, reading only, please.*
- Organize games, such as spelling bees and charades based on fairy tales.
- Play book trivia question-and-answer or create book crossword puzzles.
- With clues read over the intercom, play "Name That Book."
- Take field trips. Visit local literary landmarks, the library, or a bookstore.

Part B

Publishing in the Classroom

6

Establishing a Publishing Environment

"In creating, the only hard thing's to begin. A grass blade's no easier to make than an oak."

— James Russell Lowell

"Awesome, amazing, wonderful" — that's how some senior students at a Young Authors Conference describe their friends' publishing projects. Each year, their teacher picks a small group to attend the conference. They spend months making books, caught up in a publishing extravaganza. They brainstorm, sketch, and gather materials for their projects. By May, they're ready to go to the annual conference.

"They really blossom when they make their own books," say their teachers. "Some write fabulous collections of short stories and poems, while others create exciting picture books. It's fantastic! These kids are incredibly motivated young authors and illustrators. Many of them hope to go on in this field."

"It's so much work, but worth it," one student insists. When I asked these twelve- and thirteen-year-olds to help me target what generates their excitement for writing and illustration, this is what we came up with.

> ## Motivation for Publishing
>
> Love of books
> Knowing someone who did project well
> Independence
> Desire to receive award/recognition
>
> Self-expression
> Satisfaction
> Relaxation

The journey through the publishing process takes time and patience. The factors that help and hinder it are outlined next.

The Publishing Process	
Things That Help It	Things That Hinder It
Practice	Lack of time
Support	Lack of confidence
Competition	Lack of trust and respect for
Having an excellent teacher	the teacher
Desire	Having something better to do
Having basic materials	Fear
Courage, passion, and conviction	

The positive factors all relate to the creation of a supportive atmosphere, which is essential to sparking enthusiasm.

A Place for Publishing

The Partnership Principle

Being a partner with the teacher-librarian means sharing the responsibilities as well as the rewards. Ideally, everyone takes an interest in the quality of student work. It's a win-win situation. Librarians can help with publishing projects, particularly in recommending resources and in handling new technologies. As part of your mandate, learn how to use equipment such as scanners and cerlox-binding machines. Then see that volunteers and students get trained on new systems so that data can be accessed whenever needed. Computers give students access to information, as well as opportunities to be original and highly productive.

Some schools have a central place, usually a spare room or the resource centre, where students, teachers, and parent volunteers work together to publish books. This, of course, is the natural spot for photocopy machines, scanners, laminating machines, computers, and printers — all of which can help produce professional-looking projects.

Other schools have more decentralized publishing programs. They may have self-contained classroom programs, where students produce wonderful books without sophisticated equipment. Or, schools may publish on a project basis, working with the librarian or resource teacher: part of the project is done in the classroom and part in the school library or computer lab.

No model is better than another. Resources vary from school to school, depending on needs and priorities. What matters most is that some writing be done by each student every day. Since we know that children begin school with little or no writing experience, we want to ensure that they get practice: practice in writing about experiences and ideas that are real and relevant to them.

The publishing environment described in the next few pages may be used to encourage the production of books in all curriculum areas, including social studies, science, and the arts. As such, publishing extends beyond the "language arts" period.

Creating the Right Atmosphere

Teachers convey messages to students by the environment they create for them. For example, if you display children's writing or art around the room, you are telling them that you value their creativity. If children's books line your shelves, you show your love for reading. The importance of the teacher's involvement cannot be underestimated.

The ideal publishing environment offers students a mix of guidance and freedom. If you create conditions that promote writing and picture-making as important forms of self-expression, you will help to provide stability, challenge, and interest for your students. To establish a good publishing atmosphere, you must guarantee that space, materials, and time are used in ways that encourage kids.

Space

Before you launch into any publishing activities, think about your classroom layout.

- Aim to develop a publishing centre where students can create and where you have room for large and small group learning. Make a variety of basic materials, such as paper, writing tools, and resource books, easily available to students. (See "The Best Publishing Resources for Students," pages 68–69.)
- Provide comfortable places to read and write.
- Set up a table or bulletin board on which you highlight a professional author or illustrator. Feature work by the creator, tips, photographs, letters, profiles, and Web site information.
- Display examples of writing and pictures by teachers, parents and students, as well as selections from books and magazines.

And don't forget about the role of halls and walls in nurturing students. "Walls can teach," says Stephanie Harvey, author of *Nonfiction Matters*. "In classrooms that value inquiry . . . topics, questions, sign-up sheets and kids' work cover the walls." As noted in Chapter 3, you can use your halls and walls to convey messages about reading, writing, and creativity. Think of your bulletin boards as powerful motivational tools!

Materials

To set up a publishing area in your classroom, make the following staples handy for student use:

- ❏ a computer with word-processing and publishing software;
- ❏ off-white lined paper for writing drafts and white paper for final copy;
- ❏ pencils, erasers, pencil crayons, thin-tipped markers, water color and poster paints;
- ❏ heavy cardboard, bristol board;
- ❏ scraps (paper, ribbon, thread, cloth);
- ❏ darning needles and string or wool;
- ❏ different colors and sizes of paper, including construction paper and wallpaper samples;
- ❏ scissors, tape, and glue for cutting and pasting;

Publishing Slogans

Promote publishing on your walls. Headings like these help students make connections.

Good Reading Is the Key to Good Writing

Every Child an Illustrator

Storytelling through the Arts

Read to Write!

Writers' Wisdom

Tips from the Pros

Picture This!

Read to Succeed

Read 'Em and Reap

□ index cards;

□ paper clips and Post-it notes on which you can write comments and questions;

□ stapler, brass fasteners;

□ reference materials such as dictionaries, grammar handbooks, and how-to guides on writing and illustrating for children;

□ samples of students' finished work.

FEATURE: The Best Publishing Resources for Students

Just as good cooks rely on recipes to help them make great-tasting food, children need resources to help them become better at writing and picture-making. A variety of excellent books and software is available.

How-to books for children

* *Draw and Write Your Own Picture Book*, by Emily Hearn and Mark Thurman

  Lettering styles, cover designs, and points of view are among the topics explored. Children learn how to create their own picture books with step-by-step instructions using storyboarding techniques.
* *Fun-tastic Collages*, by Mark Thurman

  This book encourages students to recycle and arrange paper to make posters, book covers, and illustrations. It includes lessons on how to draw shadows, faces, in perspective, and more.
* *The Grammar Handbook for Word-Wise Kids: Basic English Grammar, Punctuation and Usage*, by Gordon Winch and Gregory Blaxell

  Here is an introduction to the parts of the speech, sentences, phrases and clauses, and punctuation, all of which will help kids learn to make sense of their writing and speaking.
* *How to Plan Your Drawings*, by Mark Thurman

  Simple instructions teach children how to draw from different points of view, including bird's eye, ant's eye, close-ups, and more.
* *Looks Great!: Exciting Ways of Presenting Your Projects*, by David Deakin and Gordon Moore

  This book shows kids how to create headings, design borders, make lively letters and layouts, making everything from a single page to a whole publishing assignment look great.
* *Story Presentations: How to Turn Your Story, Project or Report into Something Amazing*, by David Kehoe, illustrated by Eric Fredrickson

  Children learn how to present their stories or reports in special ways, such as pop-ups, pyramids, accordions, and more.
* *Writing*, by Amanda Lewis, illustrated by Heather Collins

  Young readers experience all facets of writing through their five senses — by making paper, figuring out braille, writing a story, and experimenting with printing.
* *Writing Your Best Picture Book Ever*, by Kathy Stinson, illustrated by Alan and Lea Daniel

The award-winning author takes children through the steps of writing a picture book, with tips about characters, titles, dialogue, revising drafts, and more.

Publishing software

Since kids love computers and understand them better than many adults, it's no wonder that publishing software has been popping up at the elementary level. The following are a few of the more popular software packages.

• *Storybook Weaver® Deluxe* (Ages 6–14)

Children can set a mystery in their own backyard or make dinosaurs rise out of swamps. . . . They're the storytellers. Virtually anything kids imagine can happen through outrageous illustrations, sound effects, and storybooks they create.

CD-ROM WIN*/MAC**
(*8MB, 486, SVGA) **5MB, 68040, Sys. 7.1)

• *The Amazing Writing Machine®* (Ages 6–12)

Kids can create storybooks, poems, letters, and more with amazing tools like a rhyming dictionary, secret coder, and brainstorming ideas. The CD-ROM includes *Kid Pix* painting and drawing tools so kids can add their own artwork!

CD-ROM WIN/MAC**

• *Student Writing & Research Center™*

Kids can create reports and projects with this word processor and desktop-publishing tool. More than 150 clip-art pictures are included.

CD-ROM WIN
(8MB, 486/33, SVGA)

Time

Give student writers some freedom of choice in deciding both how to begin writing and what to write about. For example, one child might need to draw before writing, another may need to think for a while, and a third may begin writing immediately.

Vary the time when you have your students write. As with adults, children's energy levels change during the day. Some of your students might be bright-eyed and ready to write early in the morning. Others may find writing comes more easily later in the afternoon. "There are favorable hours for reading a book, as for writing it," observed the poet Longfellow.

Allow children sufficient time to develop their ideas. Be aware, too, that students often become frustrated if their writing time is interrupted or cut short. They need practice if they are to become effective writers.

Remember, too, not to limit publishing to any particular time or subject. It can go on throughout the day in all curriculum areas.

We all know what a difference a teacher can make in a student's development. Ultimately, if you create a supportive climate, you will spark students' enthusiasm. Here's to all teachers who recognize and nurture their students' special talents!

7

Bringing Parents into the Picture

Parents also play a key role in motivating their children to read and write. Many parents know that reading aloud is important for young children, but may not realize that it is just as important for older children. They may not know that reading to their child, even after they can read themselves, will help them to write well. The most effective writers in the world are people who have loved books and read them ever since they can remember. Unfortunately, families spend less time reading together as children get older. Often parents stop reading aloud once their children can read on their own. Encourage them to take the time.

As a teacher you want your students to develop an attitude towards writing that is positive and exciting. Remember that the most successful learning experiences are those in which teachers and parents work together.

Some parents may be unfamiliar with approaches such as classroom publishing, author studies, and Young Authors Conferences, especially if they were not taught that way. Make them aware of the philosophy behind these approaches — that these activities help stimulate writing and picture-making, which are important forms of self-expression — so that they can help foster creativity.

Forums for Reaching Parents

Establish "partnerships" with parents early in the school year. Some opportunities to seek parent support, such as Meet the Teacher Night, already exist; others, such as a monthly newsletter, you can create. Then rally with parents to encourage your kids to read and write — all year long!

> **Ways to Promote the Reading-Writing Connection to Parents**
>
> 1. At Meet the Teacher Night
> 2. In an introductory letter
> 3. In monthly classroom newsletters
> 4. In showcases, on bulletin boards, on a marquee
> 5. Via a parent resource library
> 6. At special school events

1. Meet the Teacher Night

Since some parents are unfamiliar with the concept of classroom publishing, take the opportunity to explain it at Meet the Teacher Night. The principal can set the stage by sharing with an audience the language arts vision — of which publishing is a part — for the upcoming year.

Next, you and your colleagues meet with parents in your classrooms. Briefly explain your programs and show work samples such as writing folders and published books. Let parents ask questions about programming.

2. An Introductory Letter

If you believe writers are created largely through reading, and wish to see more reading done by parents at home, say so! A letter to parents might begin with an explanation of the reading/writing connection, followed by recommendations for home reading and an outline of your program. A sample appears on the next page.

Dear Parents,

One of the greatest gifts you can give your child is time set aside for reading together. Our media-filled society provides other options for information and entertainment, but the best way to help children learn to read and write is to share books with them on a regular basis.

Reading aloud is important for kids of all ages. It helps them learn how stories work. They hear the rhythms, listen to the words, feel excited by the plots, and come to know what makes a good beginning and a satisfying ending. One of the best ways to inspire your child to write is by reading good books together. No child is too old to be read to. Please set aside several times a week for reading aloud to your child.

What books are best? Choose top quality ones: classics and award winners. Librarians and bookstore clerks can help you select good literature. Our children are lucky to have all kinds of great books to read!

Periodically, focus your reading on a particular author or illustrator. Usually you can find information about authors and illustrators on the book cover. Maybe your child would like to draw a picture or write a letter to send to the author via the publisher. Together, observe and compare styles of illustrations, and do pictures "in the style of" a favorite illustrator.

At school we will be reading books every day, learning about different authors, and making books of our own. It is important to look at how writers are created because it has so much to do with reading. Children who are learning to write and illustrate their own stories look up to authors and illustrators as role models. Most importantly, they become motivated in their own creativity.

Your support will reinforce the skills, knowledge, and attitudes that your children are developing at school.

Happy reading and writing (together),

3. A Monthly Classroom Newsletter

In *Guiding the Reading Process*, David Booth, a renowned author and educator, says all parents need to know what is going on in their child's classroom. They enjoy hearing about their child's studies and can often contribute books and other resources to enhance the learning. Newsletters are a primary tool for communication.

To help give parents a sense of their child's language activities, outline your program for the weeks ahead in the newsletter. Give an overview of the skills your students are learning. Identify the author you are studying that month so that parents can visit the library to pick up some of the author's books. List Web sites pertaining to children's books. Explain how parents can become involved with upcoming themes. Periodically, recommend good book titles to them. Also, provide a monthly calendar marking important events such as an author visit or a trip to the local library. Provide inspiring quotes about reading and writing in your newsletters — many are available in author profiles and on the Internet.

Newsletters should bubble with enthusiasm about the reading and writing skills that children are mastering at school. Kids *and* parents respond well to positive reinforcement. *Praise* them when you know reading is happening regularly at home! You can set the tone for positive thinking and belief in the creative spirit of children. Read these excerpts from a number of newsletters.

> "Thanks for your commitment to nightly reading with your children. Not only do your children have a wonderful appetite for books, but they have keen interest in publishing stories of their own."

> "Your home reading is paying off. Our classroom has been a hive of activity with students busy writing and publishing stories . . ."

And this letter which appeared within a newsletter:

Dear Parents,

Today your child is bringing home a book published by the Grade Three Creative Company. The children have learned many steps of publishing: thinking, talking, writing, proofreading, and illustrating a story. The results are dazzling!

Now the books are ready for your comments on the back page. Your positive comments to them would be most inspiring.

Please return the books after you have commented as the children will be sharing them with their peers later this week. The principal and vice-principal want to enjoy the books as well.

Happy Reading!

Sincerely,

Sharing Work Samples

Once you tell parents in the newsletter how you will send home student work, arrange to use a brown envelope with a note similar to the one below attached. The envelope can go between home and school all year long.

Dear Parents,

Your child is proud to show you his/her work. Please take time to discuss it together. Your interest can be very helpful. Then sign and send this work back tomorrow. Portfolios of students' writing and art are kept at school to help in goal setting, evaluation, and parent/teacher interviews.

Sincerely
(Your child's teacher)

Date

_____

Parent Signature

_____

Comments

_____

Kids can add to the excitement by contributing to the classroom newsletter. They might describe what they studied last month, make a forecast about upcoming activities, and share news about memorable projects they've done. Writing samples by student authors can also be published here.

Your first newsletter, probably in September, should let parents know how you plan to inform them about how their child is doing in school. You might explain that you will periodically send home work samples for them to look at, sign, and send back the next day. In that way you establish a pattern of communication.

4. Showcases, Bulletin Boards, and Marquees

You can promote the reading/writing connection to your families schoolwide with a central showcase or bulletin board. If the board is in a high traffic area, more students and parents will see it. Feature information on the following:

❑ upcoming events involving parents, such as Family Reading Night;

❑ upcoming school events, such as an author visit or a Young Authors Conference;

❑ newspaper articles pertinent to reading, writing, and art;

❑ relevant community news — library or bookstore events such as author/illustrator visits;

❑ requests for parental assistance, perhaps to listen to children read, type stories ready to be published, and help with printing, binding, and laminating in the publishing process; and

❑ examples of good student work.

Outside the school, you can continue to promote values through a marquee placed in a prominent area. Before Christmas, one school set a marquee facing a busy street with this bright message:

> THE BEST GIFT YOU CAN GIVE . . .
>
> MAKE READING WITH YOUR CHILD
>
> A DAILY HABIT.

Explains the school's principal: "We want to spread a positive message to the whole community. This is one of many ways we reinforce reading and writing. The marquee catches people's eye and makes them think."

5. A Parent Resource Library

Many schools establish a parent resource library so that parents can gain more information to help their child in reading and writing. Parent libraries can be developed over time depending on needs, issues, and funding. You can offer all kinds of excellent guides to writing and illustration in one.

According to Maureen Botrie and Pat Wenger, authors of *Teachers and Parents Together*, "A library promotes a caring climate that makes a 'welcome' statement to the whole family. It values the role of the parents in developing strong students . . . the message to students is that both the parents and educators value reading and are working toward the same goal."

Some schools set up the parent library in the resource centre. Others use the front foyer of the school, which is highly visible and accessible to parents entering the building. Botrie and Wenger recommend that the library might best be placed in a quiet corner within the office. Its presence gives a strong message to parents about valuing their needs. The office is the most open, accessible spot during most of the day. Support staff can add additional books, brochures, or magazine information to it.

Botrie and Wenger also advise: "To facilitate the lending of books, institute an honor system that assumes parents will voluntarily return the books. If parents feel trusted, the greater the chance that they will return the trust. The presence of the school secretary should jog the parents' memories to return the books. The school librarian could determine and post the length of time appropriate to keep the books (e.g., one book at a time for one month). A sign-out book should be made available."

Funding for the parent library can come from several sources, including the home and school association, book fair earnings, funds raised from a used book sale, donations, and gifts-in-kind.

Titles Related to Publishing for the Parent Resource Library

- *Art & Illustration for the Classroom: A Guide for Teachers & Parents*, by Rhian Brynjolson
- *Choosing Children's Books*, by David Booth, Larry Swartz, and Meguido Zola
- *Everybody's Favourites*, by Arlene Perly Rae
- *The Grammar Handbook for Word-Wise Kids*, by Gordon Winch and Gregory Blaxell
- *Raising Readers: Helping Your Child to Literacy*, by Steven Bialostok
- *The Read-Aloud Handbook*, revised edition, by Jim Trelease
- *The Reading Solution: Make Your Child a Reader for Life*, by Paul Kropp
- *Spelling for Parents*, by Jo Phenix and Doreen Scott-Dunne

6. Special Events

Occasionally, you may wish to organize a program night, perhaps a presentation by an author or illustrator, or a lecture or workshop intended to keep parents up-to-date on trends in education. The program can provide parents with insights about their child's learning and reinforce valued home practices, such as reading aloud and writing frequently. The guest speaker may require a fee, but the evening should be free to participants. Ideally, provide refreshments and child care, to encourage attendance.

Special events such as a Family Reading Night do far more than inform parents about the nature of a school's language arts program. They represent a culmination or fulfillment of that program — a celebration of the creative achievements of students. This matter is addressed more fully in the last chapter of the book, Celebrating the Publishing Process.

Parents as Partners in Publishing

Publishing Tips

Hockey tape works well for binding hand-sewn books.

Ask parents to save cardboard liners from packages for items like pantyhose and shirts to use as book covers.

Based on the premise that book publishing is a lot of work, there are many ways parents can help at school. If you need extra hands, here are some suggestions for involving parent volunteers:

- listening to children read their stories;
- typing stories ready to be published;
- serving as an audience for children's ideas in all publishing stages;
- selecting books at the library;
- helping with scanning, printing, binding, and laminating student work.

You might invite parents to become involved in publishing by sending a special letter home. Identify some of the roles they can play, as outlined above.

Be sure to train parent volunteers properly. Since those with computer skills may help prepare a piece of writing for display, encourage them to pay particular attention to grammar, spelling, and typing accuracy. Naturally, you will need to show parents who will be photocopying, cerlox-binding, scanning, printing, or laminating how to use school equipment.

Remember to acknowledge all parent volunteers by thanking them in your newsletters or by holding a special event such as an Appreciation Tea in June.

Now, on to a discussion of where writers get their ideas from and how you can help put these ideas into action!

8

Writing about What Interests the Writer

"Writing comes more easily if you have something to say."

— Sholem Asch

Invite your students to pretend they are all authors about to write something. You might ask, "What's the very first thing you need to have?" (Amidst the whispering you'll hear "a title!" or "a pencil.") Give them a hint: "It's starts with an 'i.'" Their answers will vary.

"Imagination."
"Illustration."
"Ink."
"Inspiration."
"Introduction."
"Intelligence."

(Ironically, all of these words involving creativity start with the letter "i.")

The word you are looking for is "idea." We need an idea to write about. All books begin with an idea. Some authors say that thinking of a good idea to write about is the hardest part of their job, but when they get one, the writing is easy. "Starting is half the battle," says fiction author Jean Little. Other authors, like Robert Munsch, have hundreds of story ideas, but find the writing tricky. It all depends on the person.

Writing about Special Interests

Topics for writing emerge from the writer's interest. While some authors create stories of make-believe, others write books because they care about certain topics, such as history, sports, or the arts. Whether they engage in non-fiction or creative writing, writers write best about things they know about or are interested in.

Bringing Creativity to Non-Fiction

Ruth Heller approaches non-fiction with an utterly unique style. In addition to using bright, beautiful pictures, she writes in rhyme! To her, rhymes lend a playfulness to subjects that may otherwise be dull. Sometimes, even her book titles rhyme, for example, *Merry-Go-Round: A Book of Nouns*. Alliteration, the occurrence of two or more words having the same sound, also helps bring dry subjects to life as in the title *Many Luscious Lollipops: A Book about Adjectives*.

Invite your students to use rhyme in a similar way. First, ask them to write simple directions, such as how to get to the office from your class. Then have them do it again — in rhyme. Add to the challenge by asking them to use alliteration in their headings!

Fiction writer Janet Lunn thinks that too often children are asked to write fiction, as though creating stories is the only way to develop their imaginations. In her opinion, that's not necessary. "Everybody's got an imagination," she says. "They just don't all work in the same way." With the use of active verbs, lively headings, and colorful descriptions, non-fiction writing can be every bit as exciting as fiction!

Writing non-fiction appeals enormously to many children. They can develop areas of special interest, such as hockey, magnetism, or dance, and publish exciting non-fiction books. Regardless of whether they decide to write fiction or non-fiction, children write best when they choose their topics.

Extending Personal Interests

When your students are thinking of writing ideas, encourage them to focus on their interests — sports, adventure, animals — and then lead them to write about them.

For example, if a child likes hockey, draw him out on the subject. He may be an expert on the National Hockey League! Suggest that he write and illustrate a book on some aspect of hockey, for example:

the history of the NHL — How did it begin? How has it changed over the years?

present organization — What teams, conferences, divisions are involved?

awards — What are they? For what are they given?

jobs in the NHL — What do coaches, trainers, managers, owners, and officials do? What other hockey jobs are there?

stars — Who are some famous past and present stars of hockey?

Bring the student's attention to book tie-ins, sources of research, for example, these titles by James Duplacey: *Hockey's Hottest Centers*, *Hockey's Hottest Defensemen*, *Hockey's Hottest Goalies*, and *Hockey's Hottest Wingers*.

Monsters are another popular interest which, if not exactly non-fiction, can be readily researched. Myths, legends, and folklore are filled with dragons, sea creatures, strange land beasts, and imaginary beings. Sasquatch, Loch Ness monster, and the Abominable Snowman are some famous monsters. If a student expresses interest in monsters, suggest that she choose one and find out about it. She could write a book on its origin, appearance, habits, and habitat, including pictures, a table of contents, and well-organized information.

Making Curriculum Connections

Non-fiction writing lends itself to specific content areas. If, for example, the curriculum identifies a topic such as pioneer life, children can write and illustrate booklets about personal interests related to that topic, perhaps Trapping, Logging, Pioneer Homes, Pioneer Crafts, Entertainment, and Community Life. In this instance, some excellent book tie-ins are the award-winning *Josepha: A Prairie Boy's Story*, by Jim McGugan, illustrated by Murray Kimber; *A Pioneer Story*, a comprehensive all-in-one classroom resource by Barbara Greenwood, illustrated by Heather Collins; and *Pioneer Crafts*, also by Barbara Greenwood, illustrated by Heather Collins. Always keep an eye out for resources to share with your students.

Students can approach writing about a curriculum area in different ways. For example, if someone studying Native peoples was interested in learning more about hunting tools, he might present research through a series of diagrams with interesting information and captions.

With younger children, you may focus on People in the Community. Each child can choose one of the following people who work in the community, write about how they contribute, and make a picture.

firefighters	doctors
garbage collectors	bankers
postal workers	street cleaners
veterinarians	police officers
bus drivers	lifeguards
nurses	dentists
ministers, priests, rabbis	

Then you can bind the pages together to produce a class book. (See Cooperative Books, Chapter 9.) The *In My Neighbourhood* series, written by Paulette Bourgeois and illustrated by Kim La Fave, provides some relevant book tie-ins for this unit. Children also benefit from guest speakers and class trips, which inspire other forms of writing. For example, visiting a fire station can prompt the writing of letters of permission or thanks, observation lists, stories about the trip, directions on maps with labels in sentences, and stories about firefighters.

Older children can explore topics, such as Life in Ancient Greece, by focusing on an area of interest such as Food, Shelter, Government, Art and Architecture, Religion, or Family Roles. They can publish booklets, magazine or newspaper articles, or accounts of real events.

Writers develop fiction or non-fiction for books, magazines, trade journals, newspapers, technical studies, radio, film, TV, and advertising — or purely for pleasure. Not all material is prepared for publication. And writers tend not to lock themselves into one area. Paulette Bourgeois, for example, writes both children's picture books, such as the Franklin the turtle series, and non-fiction, including *The Amazing Dirt Book*. We cannot generalize that any form of writing is easier or more appealing than another.

What's most important is to encourage children to write about things they are interested in, to nudge them in directions that match their interests. In the next two chapters we will explore where writers get their ideas from and how they sustain creative thought.

FEATURE: First Publishing Project — Fall Picture Book

Autumn is the perfect season to kick off your publishing program. Children, notably in Grades 3 and 4, can make Fall picture books with great success. While you shouldn't routinely assign writing topics, this model breaks the process of writing non-fiction into manageable stages, and allows your students to practise the beginning skills necessary for publishing. Using this approach, you model for them how to design borders, write interesting sentences, make a table of contents, and create a cover. Then they work on their books at home. Later, they can follow this model for other projects.

Go on an autumn adventure with your students, maybe picking apples, choosing pumpkins, or hiking in nature. Set up a harvest table in the classroom, and stock it with reading treats like *Thanks for Thanksgiving*, by Heather Patterson. Use books as a starting point for your students' first publishing project of the year.

- *It's Pumpkin Time!*, by Zoe Hall, illustrated by Shari Halpern

  Readers are treated to a delightful lesson on the life cycle of a pumpkin, as a brother and sister plant a pumpkin patch. "A bumper crop of entertainment and basic know-how." — *Publishers Weekly*

- *The Seasons of Arnold's Apple Tree*, by Gail Gibbons

  Here's a factual account of the seasonal changes a boy's apple tree undergoes. "The adventure aspect and the special features (such as the apple pie recipe) will undoubtedly hold a child's interest." — *Science Books and Films*

- *Red Leaf, Yellow Leaf*, by Lois Ehlert

  Bright collages illustrate this introduction to the life of a tree as it matures through the seasons. "A glorious contribution to non-fiction shelves." — *Booklist*. Boston Globe/Horn Book Award for Non-fiction. Outstanding Science Trade Book for Children

- *Thanks for Thanksgiving*, by Heather Patterson, illustrated by Mary Jane Gerber

  Glowing illustrations and simple rhyme celebrate the pleasures of fall and family that lie at the heart of Thanksgiving.

Gather your students together in the group meeting area. Explore autumn by asking open-ended questions: "What do you know about Autumn?" "What are some signs of Autumn?" Record their responses.

Categorizing follows brainstorming. Ask children to categorize ideas about autumn that belong together and create headings for each group of words: "People Preparing for Fall," "Harvest," "Fall Sports," "Animals Getting Ready for Winter." Then use their categories to create a project outline. A sample outline follows.

Autumn is apples and pumpkins, pies and harvest moons . . .

Fall Picture Book Project

Here is a picture book project for Fall. Find pictures for each topic listed below. Use magazines, cards, or photographs, or draw pictures yourself. Give each page a heading or title. Write three to five interesting sentences to describe each picture and put an attractive border around it. Number the pages and put them in order.

1. People	raking leaves, visiting fall fairs, picking apples, going on nature hikes . . .
2. Animals	squirrels gathering nuts, birds flying south . . .
3. School	new classmates, new teacher, new clothes, school bus . . .
4. Harvest	golden wheat, vegetables, pickling, corn, canning . . .
5. Trees	leaves turning color, country scenes . . .
6. Television	new fall shows . . .
7. Sports	baseball, soccer, football, road hockey . . .
8. Special Days	Hallowe'en: goblins, witches, ghosts, pumpkins . . . Thanksgiving: turkey, pumpkin pie, vegetables . . .

After you finish the inside pages, design a cover and table of contents. Here are some helpful hints for making them.

Cover	*Table of Contents*
Use sturdy paper.	List each heading.
Put a title in large neat letters.	Add a page number beside each
Include a picture.	heading.
Provide your name.	

A Message from Heather Patterson, author of *Thanks for Thanksgiving:*

"When I taught Grade Three, I would ask the kids to tell me about things they are thankful for. They would give me the sweetest answers and we would list them on chart paper. This gave me the inspiration to write *Thanks for Thanksgiving*. It has simple words and rhyming couplets. It's a positive thing to be observant, to be objective, to celebrate the change of season and nature."

9

Where Writers Get Ideas From

Where do writers get their ideas from? Because they are asked the question so often, most authors try to explain sincerely how they begin their books. Have your class think about where writers come up with ideas. You may cite examples from the following list to support their views.

Ten Top Ways to Get Writing Ideas

1. Other books and stories
2. Adaptations of traditional songs
3. Childhood memories
4. Imagination
5. Dreams
6. Families
7. Friends
8. Real life, current events, unexpected events
9. Places we go
10. TV and movies

1. Other Books and Stories

One of the best ways to inspire your students to write is by reading good books together. Read books by a wide range of authors to develop a sense of various styles of writing and the strengths of each. Kids can experiment with techniques that are new to them such as retelling classic tales.

Retelling traditional tales — myths, legends, folk tales, and fairy tales — is popular with children. It can be done in a serious way, or as a satire or parody.

The Appeal of Folk Tales

Aubrey Davis is a storyteller and teacher who has developed an oral language and storytelling program for developmentally challenged children. He has retold three tales in book form.

- *Bone Button Borscht*, illustrated by Dušan Petričić A beggar teaches poor villagers what can be accomplished with a few buttons and a little cooperation in this variation on the Stone Soup theme.

- *The Enormous Potato*, illustrated by Dušan Petričić Davis recounts the hilarious efforts of a family, plus a dog, a cat, and a mouse, to free an overgrown potato from the ground. This story is based on "The Enormous Turnip."

- *Sody Salleratus*, illustrated by Alan and Lea Daniel A simple trip to the store for sody salleratus (baking soda) turns into a disappearing act for a boy, a girl, an old man, and an old woman. This retelling is reminiscent of "Three Billy Goats Gruff."

Davis asserts: "Folktales give us hope. They show us that we can succeed in spite of apparent problems — and they entertain. Perhaps this accounts for their universal appeal and their amazing ability to survive."

Retelling tales in a serious way gives children practice using descriptive language without having to develop a new story. Some children will write short, simple sentences, while others experiment with more complex structures and interesting vocabulary, adding their own flavor to the story.

Begin by reading the story aloud. If you are studying ancient civilizations, read some myths, such as Greek ones, aloud, then encourage students to write and illustrate a retelling of their favorite myth. For younger children, read folk tales, such as "Little Red Riding Hood," then ask them to choose their favorite and write a new version.

Some authors, including Lydia Dabcovich, Celia Barker Lottridge, and Tololwa Mollel, have turned to the oral storytelling tradition for inspiration. They have written books based on outstanding folk tales they have discovered and told. Here are a few to watch for:

- *The Name of the Tree*, by Celia Barker Lottridge, illustrated by Ian Wallace
- *The Polar Bear Son: An Inuit Tale*, retold and illustrated by Lydia Dabcovich
- *Ananse's Feast: An Ashanti Tale*, by Tololwa M. Mollel, illustrated by Andrew Glass

The books introduce stories from other cultures to new audiences.

Some retellings approach classic fairy tales with satire and humor, and end up changing the stories significantly. Children love *The True Story of the Three Little Pigs* as told by A. Wolf, namely, Jon Scieszka. The book's satire catapulted Scieszka to international fame, along with illustrator Lane Smith. Older students particularly enjoy the humor in their award-winning *The Stinky Cheese Man and Other Fairly Stupid Tales*, which includes stories such as "Chicken Licken," "The Really Ugly Duckling," "The Tortoise and the Hair," "Cinderumpelstiltskin," and "Little Red Running Shorts." Many teachers read Jon Scieszka's books and then ask their whole class to write fractured fairy tales.

Traditional tales that take a twist are fun to read, but often difficult to write. Not every child can put a spin on a story! Try this alternative: after you have read several fairy tales together, ask your students to choose one of the characters listed below. Have them write the famous fairy tale from that character's point of view.

The giant in "Jack and the Beanstalk"	The beast in "Beauty and the Beast"
The prince in "Cinderella"	The wolf in "Red Riding Hood"
The wicked witch in "Hansel and Gretel"	The pea in "The Princess and the Pea"

Spin-a-story is yet another alternative. Make a chart that has three dials with spinners on them. Around the first dial, put the names of six or eight characters, such as Thumbelina, Puss in Boots, and Rumpelstiltskin. Around the second dial, list objects such as rollerblades, a wallet, a budgie. Around the third dial, show locations: a telephone booth, a snowtubing park, a soccer field. The items may be realistic or comical.

Invite each student to spin the dials and construct a story or poem using the character, object, and place identified.

FEATURE: Cooperative Books

Two heads are often better than one.

For example, Jon Scieszka and Lane Smith work together on many books. Scieszka writes something, and Smith draws a picture to go with it. They complement each other really well. Let your students team up with a friend — they like having that privilege — and try publishing a book together, too.

Sometimes, writers co-author a book. Robert Munsch and Michael Kusugak did this for an Inuit story called *A Promise Is a Promise*. Similarly renowned children's writer Bill Martin, Jr., thinks that having a creative partner can make for a better book. He and co-author John Archambault both contributed ideas and made suggestions and decisions when they did *Knots on a Counting Rope*. Some of your students may appreciate the advantage of a writing partner — encourage them to respect each other along the way.

Your students can also make class cooperative books. Typically, each student writes and illustrates one page. Once the pages are compiled in published form, send the book home with a different child each night for their parents to read. Ask the parents to write comments at the back of the book and to return it the next day for someone else to take home.

Students will put forth their best effort because they realize that their work will be read by a wide audience. Wrote one teacher in a monthly class newsletter:

> Our most recent class cooperative book, entitled "Rhyme Time with Play Clay," will be coming home with the helper of the day, so that each family will have a chance to read it and comment. The children delight in your comments! We share them as a class every morning during our Opening Exercises. Special thanks to our publishing parents, Mr. Warburton and Mrs. Engels, who helped to make the book.

You can introduce the creation of a cooperative book in any grade. Since such a project enables a class to produce a finished work in a non-competitive way, primary teachers, in particular, often choose to develop cooperative books with their classes. Here are a few ideas to pursue:

- Use the *I Spy* picture riddles, by Walter Wick and Jean Marzollo, to jump-start cooperative books based on simple, rhyming poetry. First, study the *I Spy* books carefully. Explore the pictures, find the hidden objects, and solve the riddles. Then have students work in pairs to create their own scenes. They can draw or cut out pictures for their theme, many cleverly hidden. Following the pattern in the *I Spy* books, they can write rhymes about their collages. Each pair can contribute one double-page spread to the class cooperative book.

Some Funny Fractured Tales

- *The Stinky Cheese Man and Other Fairly Stupid Tales*, by Jon Scieszka, illustrated by Lane Smith
- *The True Story of the Three Little Pigs*, by Jon Scieszka, illustrated by Lane Smith
- *The Frog Prince Continued*, by Jon Scieszka, illustrated by Steve Johnson
- *Ziggy Piggy and the Three Little Pigs*, written and illustrated by Frank Asch
- *Gordon Loggins and the Three Bears*, by Linda Bailey, illustrated by Tracy Walker
- *Simply Ridiculous*, by Virginia Davis, illustrated by Russ Willms
- *The Emperor Penguin's New Clothes*, written and illustrated by Janet Perlman
- *Cinderella Penguin*, written and illustrated by Janet Perlman

- Read counting books such as *One, Two, Buckle My Shoe*, then ask students to write counting rhymes of their own. Let them illustrate their rhymes and share them with others. Here's a student example:

> One, two,
> I like stew.
> Three, four,
> Give me more.

Cooperative books provide a wonderful way to encourage and celebrate student writing without overwhelming children by the demands of writing.

---

2. Adaptations of Traditional Songs

Picture books often spring from a song or a tale from a different language. That's how Phoebe Gilman came up with the award-winning *Something from Nothing*. Previously recorded by popular singing trio Sharon, Lois and Bram as "I Had an Old Coat," *Something from Nothing* is an old Yiddish tale about a young boy named Joseph, whose grandfather sews his much-loved blanket into a jacket, a vest, and finally, a button. Rich layers of visual subtext accompany the words.

Here are a few other songs made into books:

- *Two by Two*, written and illustrated by Barbara Reid
- *The Wheels on the Bus*, written and illustrated by Maryann Kovalski
- *Take Me Out to the Ball Game*, written and illustrated by Maryann Kovalski
- *The Cat Came Back*, illustrated by Bill Slavin

3. Childhood Memories

Authors sometimes write about memories from their own childhood. For example, Bernice Thurman Hunter's popular "Booky" trilogy is based on her growing up in Toronto during the Depression years. *That Scatterbrain Booky*, *With Love from Booky*, and *As Ever, Booky* are written from the point of view of Beatrice — or Booky — a spirited young girl who makes the most of her life despite many hardships facing her family. Similarly, Paul Yee drew from his own experiences of growing up in Vancouver's Chinatown to write *Tales from Gold Mountain*. Celia Barker Lottridge's *Ticket to Curlew* is inspired by her childhood and her father's life on the Prairies in the early 1900s. Stories by Michael Kusugak, such as *Baseball Bats for Christmas*, come from his growing-up years in the Far North.

Jean Little also draws upon childhood memories, as in *From Anna*, bringing a unique sensitivity to her work. Growing up, Little felt partly

American novelist F. Scott Fitzgerald observed: "You don't write because you want to say something; you write because you've got something to say."

removed from the outside world, which meant that she communicated best with characters in books. She always shows compassion and understanding towards them.

Many stories come directly from our own experiences. Encourage kids to write about things that have happened to them. They can search their own memories for times when they have had a strong feeling, be it delight, disdain, disinterest, or determination, and transmit it into great stories. Some of the best books are about people's experiences.

4. Imagination

Beloved writer Beverly Cleary gets her story ideas from experience, imagination, and the world around her. As a young child she was like the irrepressible, incorrigible Ramona Quimby that so many readers can identify with! So many things around us can trigger our imaginations and fill our minds with images and words.

Phoebe Gilman, another celebrated author, describes how she came to write her first book, *The Balloon Tree*: "It was because of my daughter, Ingrid, that I became an author. When the balloon burst on a tree branch, I wished the tree would magically sprout balloons. It didn't . . . what sprouted was an idea in my head. Why not write a story about a tree that blossoms balloons?"

While authors like Beverly Cleary and Phoebe Gilman both enjoy the world of imagination, not everybody can write about comic characters and imaginary kingdoms. Many writers prefer the "real world" of current events and true-life stories to stories of make-believe.

The Muse at Work

Author Jean Marzollo says: "I can't sit down and say, 'Today I'm going to write a picture book.' When I'm stuck for an idea, I look through the files I keep. I can't make ideas happen. Ideas usually come to me while I'm doing other things."

— From *Meet the Authors and Illustrators, Volume 2*

5. Dreams

Remembering dreams can be fun and fascinating. Children can record their dreams and write notes each morning on what their dreams were about. One book tie-in is Troon Harrison's *The Dream Collector*, a captivating tale of a boy's dream-tinged adventure: the neighborhood is overrun with dreams — pirates, a knight, a dragon, a dinosaur, and more. The points that follow will help students remember their sleep-time adventures.

Tips for Keeping a Dream Diary

1. At bedtime, put a pencil and pad of paper next to your bed. As you fall asleep, tell yourself you'll remember your dreams.
2. Don't use an alarm clock. Wake up naturally.
3. Think hard. When you first wake, lie with your eyes closed and quietly concentrate on the first thoughts in your mind.
4. Now sit up and jot down your thoughts. Start with names or phrases you remember from your dream, then add feelings and other details.
5. Date each entry.
6. Draw your dream. Include as many details as you can remember in your picture. Dream on!

6. Families

Stories are in every family! Many authors and illustrators look to family members when creating new books. For example, Kathy Stinson's own two children have provided inspiration for her stories. *Red Is Best* grew out of her daughter's stubornness about wearing her red stockings. *Big or Little* was inspired by her son, who could feel very grown up remembering his library card, but very small forgetting to do a chore for his mother.

Phoebe Gilman explains how the idea for *The Wonderful Pigs of Jillian Jiggs* came from one of her daughter's ventures: "My daughter had made some little mice bookmarks and everybody loved them, so she and her girlfriend decided to go into business. It was a great success! Each mouse was different, each one had a name and each one was special. By the time they were finished, the girls didn't want to sell any of them. In the end, they kept them all for themselves! To me, this sounded like a perfect story . . . it sounded like something Jillian Jiggs would do."

Students may enjoy telling some of their own family stories, perhaps about a sibling's habits, a family member who lives far away, a favorite family activity, or a special relationship they have with a family member. Many kids have interesting stories about their past and present lives. We should encourage them all to value their heritage.

Some children may not know they have a family story to tell. Suggest a few questions they can ask parents: What was it like when you were kids? What can you tell me about my grandfather? Did you ever get into trouble as a kid — how? Questions like these will prompt stories and maybe even books of special meaning. Students might prepare a family history, with a family tree, pictures of family members, and interesting information about each person; or a cookbook, with favorite family recipes along with stories, drawings, and photographs; or a story about their parents, with headings such as When My Parents Were Kids, The Funniest Thing That Ever Happened to My Parents, Things My Parents Are Good At, and Things I Will Try to Do When I Am a Parent.

7. Friends

Angel Square (Brian Doyle), *A Friend Like You* (Roger Paré), the Frog and Toad series (Arnold Lobel) . . . some of the best books for kids are based on the joys and pitfalls of friendship. Students, too, can write stories about friendship and add pictures to their books.

8. Real Life, Current Events, Unexpected Events

True-life stories are so popular with kids that National Geographic's *World* magazine for children features one in nearly every issue! Such stories tell of lives which are full of action, or tragedy, or fun, or triumph and range from a wide variety of experiences such as battling Mt. Everest to contending with American slavery.

Many children prefer to write about real people and events. Invite them to compile photo and word essays on key figures in the world today or to turn a current event into a tall tale.

Unplanned events — a wasp in your classroom, the first snowfall — add riproaring excitement and may also prompt writing activity. That's often how poet Jack Prelutsky gets his creative juices flowing for books like *It's Snowing! It's Snowing!*

9. Places We Go

Artists and writers often talk about the power of observation in their work. Many of them carry notebooks to record what they observe in their travels. Graeme Base's *The Eleventh Hour*, a complex mystery story with lavish illustrations, was based on observations Base made while on a trip around the world. Sketches of interesting things he saw and experienced became valuable records for the book.

Brenda Clark, illustrator of Franklin the turtle books, says: "When I'm not illustrating, I go hiking, canoeing and cycling with my husband and son. When we go outdoors I get lots of ideas for things to put into my paintings such as how the water and sky look at different times of the day, or the many types of flowers, trees, plants and even houses there are around me." She recommends: "An illustrator should be very observant. It helps to keep a sketch book of the interesting things you see every day." Children can record things they observe when they go places, and then write a story based on those things.

Writing about What You See

"Elephant seal pups are fun to watch and sketch," says Rosie Records of Petaluma, California. For years, Rosie has studied elephant seals, sea-dwelling mammals that can weigh up to two tons each. From December through March the seals "haul out" of the water to breed on a beach near her home. She wrote and illustrated a book about them called *Haul Out: Elephant Seals at West Drakes Beach, Point Reyes National Seashore.*

Visitors watch the seals through telescopes at the park. Once hunted to near extinction, the seals are now protected and are making a comeback. People must observe them from a distance. "I did most of my sketches through the 'scopes," says Rosie. "I enjoyed capturing the animals' expression and behaviour. I also worked hard to write precisely about them. It was very satisfying."

— From *World* magazine

Books Children Can Make

There are all kinds of books children can develop as publishing projects. Here are some of them: flip books, recipe books of favorite dishes, poem collections, photograph books, trip books, observation logs (usually of animals), song books, puzzle books, "I remember" books, monster books, books about "us," guide books to the school, guest books, address and telephone books for their friends, joke books, autobiographies, pattern books, comic books, and novels.

10. TV and Movies

Sometimes, writers get ideas for stories when they watch TV. Remember the TV show called *MASH*? On *MASH* there was a character named Hawkeye who got claustrophobia every time he went into small, dark places. In one episode Hawkeye said, "If I were a turtle, I'd be too scared to go in my own turtle shell!" That's what gave Paulette Bourgeois the idea to write *Franklin in the Dark*, her first Franklin story.

Now, Franklin is a celebrity of international children's culture. The popular turtle stars in numerous books available to kids all over the world — including Japan, Australia, Belgium, and England. There are also Franklin plush toys, puppets, CD-ROMs, videos, and a television series. That's what happens sometimes when somebody gets a good idea to write about!

It's fascinating to learn how books get started. All the different ways described in the preceding pages may be used to encourage student writing. So make a point of exploring where authors get their ideas from. It may help get your kids' creative juices flowing!

10

Strategies to Help Sustain Creative Thought

Playing around with Ideas

British author Roald Dahl says: "Writing doesn't just happen, it must be made to happen through hard work. You just start with a germ of an idea, a tiny germ . . . a chocolate factory? Suddenly you know it's going to fascinate children and you build around that. Or on a tree — a peach . . . a peach that goes on growing . . . a peach that just doesn't stop growing. You never see the whole landscape of the story. You work it out and play around with it. You doodle . . . you make notes . . . it grows, it grows . . ."

"Having imagination, it takes you an hour to write a paragraph that, if you were unimaginative, would take you only a minute. Or you might not write the paragraph at all."

— Franklin P. Adams

Writers write all the time. They keep journals, they write letters, they make lists . . . They do not publish everything they write! Sometimes they get frustrated and put the story away. Some stories never get finished. Whether you are a new writer or an experienced writer stuck on a curve, these are the realities of the creative process.

The same holds true for your young writers. Children learn to write by doing the same things as professionals: thinking of an idea, writing a rough copy or first draft, sharing and getting feedback and, perhaps, revising and publishing their work. If they are able to publish one book each year, they're doing well!

Be careful in assessing students' approaches to writing. An imaginative seven-year-old boy once wrote — on his own accord — a wonderful, descriptive story about baseball, his favorite team sport. The content and style were excellent. He had obviously surpassed all the writing mechanics appropriate to his grade level. Throughout his story, he used dialogue, quotation marks, and paragraphing correctly. Yet, on his report card, the teacher marked his ability to write a few simple, connected sentences as "Weak." She explained to him that his ideas were great, but that when she had given the class twenty-minute timed "tests" with designated writing topics, he was too slow at getting started.

If necessary, find ways to help students get started writing. We all know the child who, after several minutes, has written nothing on his page. When we ask him why he hasn't written anything, he mutters, "I can't think of anything to write about!" Getting stuck is frightening for a writer. Your job is to help children see possibilities.

Overcoming nervousness and fear

In the beginning most writers lack confidence. They worry about not being able to do it right, or do it well. Experience does make a difference. The best thing you can do is offer your students lots of opportunities to write, with patience, understanding, and help along the way.

Award-winning writer Norma Fox Mazer admits that she used to write in a state of fear because she wasn't sure if she was any good. For her, it was terrifying to have nothing there to work on, to have it all swimming in her head. Experience has taught her to write down phrases and fragments as she begins a new story. Now in the first draft she pays less attention to punctuation, spelling, or grammar — what's most important is to get words down. Once she muddles her way through the first draft, she revises it, figuring things out along the way.

Author Jerry Spinelli, on the other hand, tries to get it right the first time. Unlike most of his colleagues, he doesn't rewrite much. After he writes a passage, he reads it aloud the next day. This helps him see things that he might otherwise not notice.

Use the experiences of Norma Fox Mazer and Jerry Spinelli to help students understand that we all enter stories in different ways. Creative thought is hard work, and maintaining creativity is even harder. Now that we have a sense of where writers get their ideas from, we can further explore strategies writers use to get started and sustain creative thought.

> **Six Strategies for Sustaining Creative Thought**
>
> 1. Thinking
> 2. Making interest lists
> 3. Webbing and planning stories
> 4. Sketching
> 5. Talking
> 6. Recording ideas in notebooks

1. Thinking

"Thought flies and words go on foot. Therein lies all the drama of a writer."

— Julien Green

Few writers can begin writing immediately and continue in a sustained way. For most, once they have an idea, the hard work really begins. They need time for uninterrupted thinking. Some writers find themselves so deep in thought that they can go for hours without thinking about food! Keeping focused is one of the hardest things about writing. To think well takes discipline. Many writers and illustrators say if they can't get a story the way they want, they set it aside and do something else. Then they go back and see it with fresh eyes.

With that in mind, we must encourage students to value thinking as part of the writing process. Like professional authors, some students will try to write on two or three topics before they are comfortable. They may take several days to begin their books. While they wait for ideas, we can encourage them to do other things related to their projects.

2. Making Interest Lists

Kids can keep a list of their interests in a writing folder and go to it when they need to. Develop a list of possibilities on chart paper, perhaps under this heading: Things You Like, Care About, Know a Lot About.

favorite sport	your friends
favorite hobby	where you live
a special place	the place you come from
something special you have done	your favorite animal or pet
what you would like to do when you grow up	environmental issues
yourself	your family

Then share your own interests as a model. For example, when I'm working with kids, I identify my interests: skiing, music, children's books, reading, travel, walking, and the Rocky Mountains. Now it's their turn to build an interest list. As students explore topics they care about, they come up with terrific writing ideas.

3. Webbing and Planning Stories

Some authors write a detailed outline for their books; others let the story "take care of itself." When Monica Hughes has a sense of her story, she writes an outline. To help her visualize the place she's describing, she also makes maps and charts. On the other hand, Jean Little and Beverly Cleary — two great writers — never write from an outline!

Charts, maps, webs . . . these are all means to help writers organize their ideas. Ideally, writers need to be free to express ideas, yet still be in control. One of the best techniques to try with your budding writers is webbing.

Here's one way to make a web:

1. Identify your focus (for example, classroom publishing) in the centre of the page in block letters.
2. Add circles around the focus for ideas or concepts that you know, leaving room for free association of ideas.

As an example, the web I used to help organize ideas for this book follows. Invite your students to try making a web for their next piece of writing. Model how to create a web by drawing an outline on the blackboard and explaining all the story elements. This web is a tool to help young writers to support their craft.

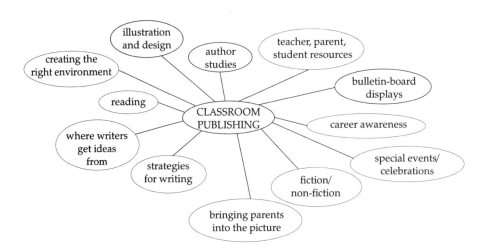

4. Sketching

Once book creators become focused on a subject, they often do some sketches. As part of the publishing process, they explore visual possibilities for a book and think them through. This way they can see the sequence of events. Doodling was a means Dr. Seuss used to summon ideas: after he drew a picture he would invent a story to explain it. The sketching technique is particularly helpful for visual learners who have difficulty writing.

5. Talking

Creativity in publishing is about the collaboration that occurs between people — the conversations that people have with one another that lead to larger volumes of ideas and, finally, results. Creativity in the classroom is about collaboration too. Giving students opportunities to interact and talk about topics, great story starters, characters, pictures, catchy titles, and satisfying endings is extremely important in liberating their creativity.

Many authors belong to writers' groups that allow them the opportunity to exchange ideas. Also, conversations and meetings with editors and publishers help writers move forward into new areas. You can draw upon a tremendous amount of creativity within your classroom by offering an opportunity for talking at teacher/student conferences, small and large group meetings, and student-to-student conferences.

As noted earlier, storyteller Robert Munsch finds it easy to generate new ideas for stories, but harder to take ideas and translate them into good stories. That's why he likes to tell his stories out loud — to interact with an audience — before he writes. He says, "We all learn to talk before we learn to write!" Just as he prefers to tell his stories first, some of your students might benefit from this approach.

Provide many opportunities for your students to talk as a lead-in to writing. Then compile their work into class books for oral sharing. Some of the topics below might provide inspiration.

What We Like to Do Best	Our Worst Nightmares
Families	Our Favorite Authors and Illustrators
Our Favorite Books	

6. Recording Ideas in Notebooks

Beverly Cleary keeps a notebook of story ideas, and as she thinks about that initial idea, others often come to her. Encourage your students to follow Beverly Cleary's lead: they can keep a notebook so that when they get an idea for a story — anything that could transport them, via their imaginations, to a new world — they write it down!

Many professional writers believe it's important to jot down ideas right away. If they don't write them down, they forget them. Encourage students to write their ideas down, too. They can save these ideas in a writing folder, and turn to their folder for inspiration. One eight-year-old boy who keeps a notebook has written down ideas about a galaxy far away, a game of baseball, and a snowtubing adventure. Perhaps those ideas will lead to exciting stories one day!

Choosing Titles

Title Attraction

Here is an exercise on creating titles for books. Take one idea listed below at a time to see how many catchy titles students can come up with. For added interest, suggest that students incorporate rhyme or alliteration in their titles.

What would you call . . .
    a book on how to make gingerbread houses?

    a story about a mystery on the moon?

    a book on how to give a haircut?

    an animal alphabet book?

    a book about snowboarding?

One of the biggest challenges for authors, editors, and publishers is to think of catchy titles for stories.

Often, publishers have "title meetings," at which everyone who has read the work — editors, sales and marketing managers — gathers to brainstorm title possibilities. Everyone brings title suggestions to the meeting. The group leader writes all the proposals on chart paper. Then everyone discusses each title, and votes on which one works best.

It is important not to judge or turn down any thoughts in the initial stage of the meeting. Brainstorming is meant to encourage creativity and divergent thinking. Sometimes, the wildest ideas make the best book titles!

Just as professionals do, some children get stuck thinking of good titles for their stories. When that happens to your students, don't have them sit there staring at a blank page for too long! Encourage them to write their story first, then think of a good title at the end. Discuss why it's important to have catchy titles, and try brainstorming to help children think of some for their stories.

Brainstorming for creative solutions

Brainstorming generates lots of ideas which lead to even more creative solutions to a given problem. It encourages children to take part in a shared, enjoyable experience, see other people's points of view, and expand their understanding of a concept. It also helps them make connections between ideas and words in a safe environment. Most importantly, it encourages creativity and serves as a springboard to divergent thinking.

Brainstorming works well when you have students who need help thinking of a good title for a story. It can be done in large or small groups. All you need are some markers, masking tape, and chart paper.

To begin, gather your students together in the meeting area. It may be useful to discuss everyone's role at the beginning. Tell your students that you need everyone's help in thinking of a good title for a story. Talk about the need for everyone to be encouraging and supportive so that you get lots of ideas. Have them read or listen to the story. Then ask them to think of a good title for the story, and record their responses on chart paper. At this time, accept all responses and make no value judgments. (You do not want to discourage any good ideas!) You may also participate, adding further ideas.

When every conceivable title suggestion has been made, ask your students why each suggestion makes a good title. Once the students explain, the other students may challenge that idea. The students must then decide to leave it or remove it. Continue with this method until you all decide which title works best.

Throughout this activity, watch for the children's ability to demonstrate knowledge of the topic, to justify their words, to think divergently, and to speak in a group.

How to run a good group meeting

Here are some tips on how to run a meeting, whether it be about a book title or another matter.

- Listen to everyone. Paraphrase, but don't judge.
- Don't put anyone on the defensive. Assume that everyone's ideas have value.
- Control dominant students without directing them.
- Realize that your interest is contagious.
- Keep everyone informed about what's expected of them. Keep notes on charts or on a board that everyone can see.
- Check with the person who owns the problem to find out if an idea is worth pursuing or if a proposed solution is satisfactory.
- Give others a turn at running the meeting. Those who learn to lead learn how to participate.

As noted before, writers write all the time. They may keep journals. They may record things that make a strong impact on them. They may take notes or write down phrases that come to them. No single approach appeals to everyone. We all communicate differently through the written word. That's why it's important to understand the various ways students tackle their work. Treat your children as individuals. Respect their particular talents and abilities!

11

Revising and Editing

Once a piece of writing is finished, an author usually works with an editor to make improvements. Sometimes the writing is shortened, sometimes parts are added, sometimes parts are changed to make the work more interesting or easier to read, and mistakes are corrected. This process is called editing. All writers, no matter how good or popular they are, need to go through the editorial process so that other people can understand and enjoy their work.

The Editor's Role

Advance, arouse, care for, cultivate, develop, encourage, excite, forward, foster, goad, incite, kindle, cause, generate, induce, nourish, nurture, prod, prompt, suggest, support, train . . . these verbs effectively describe an editor's function.

Editors, the invisible people in the publishing process, often act as a sounding board and help authors work things out. A teacher's role in the publishing process is similar to that of an editor. In many ways, you are a sounding board for your students. You also have an opportunity to nurture children in their work. If you are negative in any way, you will discourage them, possibly causing permanent damage. Kids know people are judging their work, and they are terrified of making mistakes. "I feel NERVOUS!" they say, whenever someone else reads their writing. Your students must feel good about what they've written.

- Always say something positive first: "You really grab the interest of the reader, Heather." "It's a lively story, Sarah." "Your characters are funny, Cynthia." "I like your action verbs, Steve." We want to encourage our young writers — the effects of encouragement can be long-lasting.

- After you have pointed out strengths, make a suggestion about how to improve the writing. Offer any suggestion in the form of a problem to solve: "You wrote an exciting adventure story, John! But the ending is so violent. How could you make it less brutal?"
- Teach from the bottom up, not top down. Children learn to talk before they write. When you ask them to fix something, to them it's not broken. Our emphasis needs to be less on making corrections and more on bringing children along as writers. They are learning to write, after all. We have got to keep that foremost in our hearts and minds.
- Demonstrate how to point out writers' strengths, and give your students practice in offering positive comments to their peers. Invariably, when I show children a piece of my writing, they love to point out all the errors. When it comes to commenting on a piece of writing, most of us seem conditioned to highlight the negative.
- When you're helping students edit their work, show how to build confidence by example. Be tactful! Give them ways to improve their work, rather than highlight their mistakes. Don't say, "You spelled garbage wrong!" Say, "Garbage is spelled g-a-r-b-a-g-e." Instead of "This doesn't make sense," try "This might make more sense if . . ."

Everyone has a teacher who influences his or her life. Jean Craighead George won the Newbery Medal, the award given to the author of the best American children's book published in a given year. She acknowledges the role of one teacher: "I shall never forget Mrs. Clarke. If she had scolded me — I was so unsure of myself — I would never have written again. Instead, she gave me books of verse to read, assigned me more writing than math, and — I kept writing."

Remember how deeply your words and deeds can affect young learners.

Shared Purpose

A great relationship between an author and editor is usually marked by shared values and trust. It's not good enough to shake hands, go away, and expect great creativity at the end of the process!

Similarly, one of the winning aspects of a teacher-student relationship and the work that comes out of it is when teachers are invited into the process. "Do you want to read my story?" "How do you like my picture?" You have to be there to help inspire, motivate, clarify, and lend perspective. Writing isn't some magical process whereby students get an assignment and then disappear to do it. Students produce better work when a sense of mutual trust, respect, and ownership of what is being created prevails.

Once, my Grade 3 class and their Grade 8 writing buddies collaborated in making picture books. A team of parent volunteers helped by reading and typing the children's stories. Later, we celebrated the children's books by hosting a Family Reading Night at school. There, one of my eight-year-old boys who loved to draw, but struggled with reading

Editorial Roles

In publishing, editors play different roles and several editors may work on one project. An *acquisitions* editor evaluates manuscripts or proposals and makes recommendations to the publisher. A *developmental* editor works on a project from proposal or rough manuscript to the final version. A *structural* editor clarifies and reorganizes content and structure. A *stylistic* editor eliminates jargon and smooths language. A *copy* editor checks grammar, spelling, punctuation, and consistency. And a *proofreader*, as the last person to read the whole project before publication, offers perspective and ensures that the typeset pages are error-free.

leapt up and called out as an ultimate expression of satisfaction: "That's my book!" And so it was, as surely as if he had done it all by himself. That kind of proprietary commitment makes a big difference, maybe all the difference. And, by the way, the process should be fun!

Classroom teachers play various roles in the writing process. Remember, the key to your role is to create an emotional place where young writers can be brave.

Responding to the First Draft

An author's first attempt results in a draft where the focus is on expressing ideas. Many professional authors who belong to groups such as a writers' circle discuss their work with peers. They find it helpful to get input from other perspectives and some like feedback from children's points of view. Often the draft takes several phases of reading, discussion, and conferring.

Similarly, the focus of a child's first draft should be on expressing ideas. It is inadvisable to comment on punctuation, sentence structure, grammar, or spelling at this stage. Encourage students to discuss their writing with others in order to clarify or extend their ideas. The opinions of the teacher, an older student, classmates, and family can often be helpful. Again, take a constructive approach that focuses on assessing ideas. Overemphasis on language errors can inhibit a writer from taking risks.

A Fresh Point of View

Authors often rewrite and polish a story to improve it. One way to do this is by talking to someone about the topic. Ask students to choose drafts from their writing folders and pair them up so that they will get helpful comments about their work.

The three wishes

Here's a great way to focus on expressing ideas, without overwhelming young writers with too many changes. After you read the first draft, accentuate the positive, then choose three aspects of the story where you can help make recommendations:

I wish we could think of a catchier title for this story.
I wish you could tell us more about this character.
I wish we could think of a more satisfying ending.

Revising

Explain to your students that authors go through several steps to take an original idea as far as a piece of writing ready to be shared with others. Each step helps make the author's ideas easier to understand. The whole purpose of writing, after all, is to communicate ideas. If children understand the importance of clear communication, they will accept revising as part of the writing process more readily.

The Joy of Revising

Newbery Medal winner Cynthia Voigt sees revision as part of the writing process.

"I assume that the way it (the manuscript) looks the day I finish it is not the same way it will look four months down the road," she writes. Years ago, her editor told her, "The great thing is not so much to love to write as to learn to love revision." When she first began writing, Voigt was convinced that smart people don't make rough drafts or revise, and do know the biggest words. She has since come to realize that both of her assumptions were foolish.

Voigt now enjoys the process of revision. "It's hard and satisfying in a different way than writing." When she's writing something, she says, she always feels anxious that the story might not be working. But when she's revising, she knows she's polishing a story that has already succeeded to a certain degree. "I look it over and try to figure out how to make it clearer." (Adapted from *Meet the Authors and Illustrators*, Volume 2)

Tell your students that, with all the revisions an author's work goes through, it often takes one to two years to write a book. You can cite the following examples of how authors revise:

- Marc Brown begins his Arthur books by writing rough ideas and drawing sketches. He rewrites the words for a story several times after discussion with his editor, who suggests ways of making the book more interesting.
- Rewriting is Judy Blume's favorite part of the process! She is usually terrified of writing the first draft, but once she's done so she begins rewriting immediately.
- Newbery Medalist Beverly Cleary revises some parts six times. She believes in setting the story aside for a few days so that she can see it with fresh eyes.
- Another Newbery Medalist, Betsy Byars, writes the first draft on a computer, but does her revisions by hand. She likes to write the middle of a chapter first, then, when she revises, she adds the beginning and end of the chapter.
- Tomie de Paola first writes a lot in his head, thinking the story through. He sends a revised second draft to his editor, who reads it and makes suggestions. They often work on the final draft together.
- Gordon Korman says writing comes fairly easily and sometimes he "gets it right the first time." He says his editor is like a "coach" who maximizes his creative talents.

Demonstrate revision for your students by writing passages on the blackboard and rewriting certain phrases. Children need clear-cut ideas to make their stories better. Here are some ways that work well.

Ideas for Revising

Create a beginning that grabs the reader.

Add details, especially ones that appeal to the five senses, to help the reader visualize what's happening.

Change dull verbs to livelier verbs.

Use dialogue to enhance the story.

Show how characters feel by bringing readers into their thoughts.

Organize paragraphs in a logical order.

Cut words or phrases that don't work.

Present each idea separately as a mini-lesson. Another way to teach revising strategies is to use student drafts. Each day, ask a volunteer to share a writing passage as a model, and then discuss what can be done to improve it. Once students have solid ideas to act upon, they are motivated to experiment with their own writing.

Making revising easier

Here are several tips for making it easier for your students to revise their writing.

1. Ask your students to skip lines or double-space when they write their first drafts. This will help them make additions and changes more effectively.
2. Tell your students not to take time erasing on rough drafts. Instead, ask them to cross out unwanted words.
3. Teach students how to cut and paste passages on the computer, or tell them to use tape if they are writing by hand, so that they can concentrate on the revisions.

Editing

After students finish revising, they need to proofread their work. Any piece of writing that will be brought to the final copy stage must be checked carefully for spelling, grammar, and punctuation. Proofreading is an integral part of writing.

Teach students to critically reread their own work one line at a time — this is called line-for-line editing. Show them how to cover their page with another sheet of paper so that they can concentrate on each line, even each word and letter. Suggest that they exchange work for editing, being sure to accentuate the positive. And advise them to read their work out loud because sometimes they may hear things they want to change. They should keep rough copies of their writing in folders as a record of progress.

Some students find it hard to recognize their mistakes. Here are some helpful guidelines.

Things to Look For When You Edit

1. If you don't know how to spell a word, circle it and look it up later in the dictionary.
2. Make sure that every sentence begins with a capital letter and ends with a punctuation mark.
3. Shorten long, run-on sentences.
4. Avoid unnecessary words.
5. Add missing words.

Proofreading like professionals

Model how to use proofreaders' marks — symbols to show changes that need to be made. Explain to your students that these standard marks are used by everyone who works in publishing. These symbols can help your students revise their work. Children love to use them once they know how. Introducing them in your classroom will help your students consider themselves serious writers.

Tightening a Story

1. Keep paragraphs short.
2. Use plain, everyday language.
3. Cut vague modifiers, such as very, really, and fairly.
4. Check for overuse of "he said" and similar constructions.
5. Use active verbs more than passive ones.

Editing Principles

1. Read a story three times (i) to check content, (ii) to edit, and (iii) to clean up.
2. When something is unclear, get it explained or chop it.
3. Suggest improvements to the writer, perhaps an example, specific details, or a quote.
4. Change copy if you have a good, explainable reason.

Here is one suggestion to hone
your students' proofreading
skills. Every day, write a short
passage with deliberately
made mistakes on the
blackboard and invite students
to help you mark it up. Here is
a sample.

Dear girls and boys
i love reading your stories you
all such wonderful ideas! This
is an exercise editing. I bet yuo
ar ex perts. I admire you for
haveing the courage to turn
your rough copy into master
piece.

Congratulations

You can create a classroom chart or give each student a list of the common marks for their portfolios. A chart of basic proofreaders' marks appears next as a blackline master.

Help from Computers

If your students are using computers for writing, that's great! Their experience will help them and make your life simpler, too. Here's why.

- Self-editing is easier with a word processor. Tools such as a spell-checker, grammar checker, and thesaurus help students to correct their work. (However, in keeping with the idea that writers should focus on generating ideas during the drafting phase, advise students not to get distracted by such tools then.) When spelling and vocabulary are learned in context, learning is more significant.
- Since most children like technology, they tend to spend more time on projects done on the computer.
- Children can search for information to enhance their projects.
- Many Web sites provide assignment help which motivates students.
- Technological savvy contributes to positive self-esteem.
- Computer printouts look professional.

Checking Spelling: Encourage your students to use the spellchecker to find typos and misspelled words. They should be sure to proofread the text themselves though: it's easy to type something that is a real word, but not the correct word, for example, "garbage" instead of "garage."

Encourage students to print a hard copy of their work for proofreading. The eye can see more that way. And students need to know whether their software features British or American spelling — and which spelling is acceptable for schoolwork.

Using the Grammar Checker: This program examines text for the way it follows the rules of grammar, as well as for sentence length and readability.

Looking Up Words in the Thesaurus: Students can use the thesaurus to look up synonyms and antonyms of words in their document. The thesaurus can replace the old word with the word they choose.

Basic Proofreaders' Marks

If you are working with double-spaced pages, you can mark the text directly. If pages are single-spaced or typeset, mark where you want to make a correction in the text and place the correction in the margin.

Mark	Meaning	Example
♀	Delete letters and words.	a ~~very~~ wonderful book
∧	Add letters and words.	I like funny sto∧ies.
tr	Transpose letters or words.	orignial
⌢	Delete space.	brain storm
#	Add space.	Art isfun.
≡	Capitalize.	Mrs. green
lc	Lowercase.	I have Good ideas.
¶	Start a new paragraph.	¶ "Hey!" he called.
sp. or ⬭	Check spelling.	I like funy stories.
⌄ ⌄	Add quotation marks.	It's done, she said.
⊙	Add period.	The book is good
∧,	Add comma.	I like funny short stories.

Ten Questions for Young Editors to Consider

1. Is the title catchy?
2. Who is going to read my writing?
3. Is there one main idea?
4. Does it make sense?
5. Are my ideas in the right order?
6. Have I used interesting words that readers will enjoy?
7. Have I used some examples or illustrations to help explain my ideas?
8. Is my ending good?
9. Are there any spelling and punctuation errors?
10. What about neatness?

A final word on revision and editing. All writers have an emotional attachment to their work, especially in the early stages. Sometimes we volunteer word changes and sometimes we find it tough to change certain parts. If a student declines to change his or her writing, appreciate this — with the understanding that the writer has the final say. As Stephanie Harvey tells us in *Nonfiction Matters*, "The whole duty of a writer is to please and satisfy himself, and the true writer always has an audience of one."

We'll now move on to discuss illustration and design, so you can better help your students put exciting visual ideas into action.

12

Looking at Book Illustration

While visiting schools, I always pose this question to students: "How many of you like to draw?" Hands wave wildly. Their enthusiasm soars when I ask, "How many of you would like to grow up and become a book illustrator?"

Most children love art. Many of them get really excited when it comes time to illustrate stories they have written. They have great fun experimenting with markers, pencil, paper, paints, and Plasticine.

You can capitalize on this excitement by examining picture books. Studying illustration helps students develop visual literacy and appreciate the talents artists bring to their work. Rich and often surprising discoveries may lead them to read many of the magnificient picture books being made each year — and inspire them to write and illustrate stories of their own.

Rhian Brynjolson, in *Art & Illustration for the Classroom*, writes this about the importance of visual literacy:

> Students need to be "visually literate." This is not the same as what has been passively called "art appreciation." Visual art is a means of communication: as with literature, we don't merely "appreciate it," we read it, digest it, grapple with ideas, struggle with its meaning, are influenced by it. Likewise we "read" images. This requires knowledge of visual forms in art and our environment, and an understanding of the influences of design and the meaning of graphic symbols. Visual information is present in art masterpieces.

Next, we'll consider some elements you might explore.

Looking at Media

Children's books reflect the use of various media, such as pencil crayons, acrylics, oils, and watercolors. The medium highlights the tone or "feel" of the text.

Some illustrators work best in one medium suited to their style. Others use a wide range of media and vary their style to suit the subject. For example, Maryann Kovalski usually paints with watercolor, but used pen and ink for *Doctor Knickerbocker*. Publishers look for the perfect match between illustrations and text.

Invite children to find books with bright, dark, soft, warm, light, and heavy pictures. See if they can make a connection between the medium used and the effect achieved with each. If possible, see if an illustrator can come to talk about his or her work. Ask the illustrator to discuss various media.

Media Tips

Avoid oil pastels and wax crayons because they are messy and smudge easily.

Draw a pencil guideline before you cut paper.

Clean up when you are finished.

Studying Style

Let children sort books by illustration style. For kids, the most obvious difference in style is cartoon-like versus realistic pictures. Children can look for examples of each. Michael Martchenko, Marie-Louise Gay, and James Marshall bring comic styles to their work, effective in funny stories. Other illustrators, such as Chris Van Allsburg, Karen Reczuch, Janet Wilson, and Jan Brett, lean towards a realistic approach. Illustrations by Paul Morin (*The Orphan Boy*) reflect an African influence. Every artist brings unique skills and insights to the books he or she illustrates. The same story might generate very different illustrations, depending on who does them.

Look at the chart on page 34 to see how you might compare the work of different illustrators. That chart focuses on various illustrators of Robert Munsch's books, but can be readily adapted.

Visual Elements of Composition

Art is made up of color, line, shape, and texture. With these basic components a children's book illustrator creates an imaginative, visual world that fuses with the text. The arrangement of elements is known as composition. Qualities such as balance, contrast, and movement play an important role in it.

Color: This is often the element most focused on in a picture. Red, yellow, and blue are called primary colors because you can use them to mix other colors. Green, orange, and purple are made by mixing primary colors. Colors can affect mood or feeling. Hélène Desputeaux uses vibrant colors while Kady MacDonald Denton likes soft pastels to convey

When you share books with students, look at the pictures and ask a few questions:

What do you see in the picture?

What is happening?

How would you describe the pictures?

What is your favorite picture?

You can often hook kids into books with the illustrations.

warmth. Have students make designs using contrasting colors (blue/ orange, red/green, purple/yellow).

Line: This element guides our eyes across the page and suggests the mood. Line can be wide, narrow, light, dark, straight, curved, wavy, broken, long, or short. *The Cremation of Sam McGee* and *The Shooting of Dan McGrew*, both illustrated by Ted Harrison, exemplify vivid colors, bold images, and line showing movement. Harrison's singular style has earned him international acclaim.

Let your students explore line. Draw part of a line on paper. Now, have them imagine what it could be and finish the picture. For example, a band of colorful lines can suggest the feathers of a bird; a black line can become a walking stick. Alternatively, tell students to draw lines that convey emotion: happiness, sadness, anger, or tenseness.

Shape: It can be geometric or more free-flowing. All things living or man-made fit into a basic shape. Illustrators use a circular shape to make a sun, a triangle to make a duck. Point out to children the strong dominant shapes in the childlike pictures by Eric Carle. Help students fit images to shapes in other books.

Texture: This effect can be achieved in many ways and is fun for children to experiment with. Illustrators such as Mark Thurman and Ken Nutt use crosshatched pencil drawings to create texture. Barbara Reid uses combs for grass, sharp pencils for holes, and burlap over Plasticine for a rough surface. Invite children to try such techniques in their own artwork.

Questions That Encourage Kids to Think about Composition

Where is the best place to put the main character in a picture?

Which do you prefer? — pictures that are "filled in" or pictures that have lots of white space.

How do illustrators make some things look closer than others?

It's All in the Details

The illustrations in books are often filled with details that help tell the story. Sometimes, they depict a subtext imagined by the illustrator working independently of the author. For example, a close look at the artwork of Phoebe Gilman reveals the presence of subtexts that fascinate readers.

By examining details, students learn how illustrators show movement, use colors for contrast, make an animal's fur look hairy, add shading to give depth to a picture, and more. Ask readers to look at pictures to see if they offer clues to the setting and characters in a story. Questions such as "Where do you think this scene is?" and "How do you think the character is feeling in this picture?" focus on the details.

After Phoebe Gilman finished working on *The Balloon Tree*, which took her fifteen years to write, she missed it. "So when I did *Jillian Jiggs*," she said, "I hid a little of *The Balloon Tree* in the art. There's a picture on the wall in Jillian's room that's from *The Balloon Tree*." And in *The Wonderful Pigs of Jillian Jiggs*, there's a scene where all the pigs are sitting around the table having a tea party; if you look closely, you will see that the tabletop is the Balloon Tree book. Now, every time Phoebe Gilman makes a new book, she hides all of her books in the art of her newest story.

Details in illustrations also reflect types of clothing worn at a certain time, types of housing, vegetation, and wildlife. Invite students to look for this kind of information.

Explain to your students that the level of detail depends on the intended audience. If they were illustrating a book for babies, for example, they would want to create simple pictures in bright colors. Books for older children, on the other hand, suit more complex art.

Recognizing Variety

Let your students know that one of the jobs of a good illustrator is to add lots of variety to a book. Each page should be a surprise to the reader. Discuss why this is important, leading to the idea that you want to keep the reader interested.

Show children different types of pictures and perspectives in books, including close-ups, pages with several small pictures, illustrations that cover a full page, and pictures with word balloons.

Some illustrators incorporate variety in their work by showing scenes from different angles, or points of view. Looking straight on at a scene is called a horizontal view. Looking down on a scene is known as a bird's eye view. Conversely, looking from the ground up at a scene is called an ant's eye view. Sometimes, illustrators want to show how a character is feeling — that's when they would use a close-up of the character's face.

To demonstrate points of view, use Mark Thurman's *Illustration Ideas*. Each page features giant samples of each angle, as well as cover designs, lettering styles, storyboarding, and more. You can display the twenty-four poster-size pages on your walls for all kinds of design possibilities. Other outstanding books in the series include *Draw and Write Your Own Picture Book*, *Fun-tastic Collages*, *Helping Kids Draw & Write Picture Books*, and *How to Plan Your Drawings*.

After students are familiar with the various points of view, invite them to look for views in picture books. Encourage them to try these perspectives when illustrating their own stories. That way they can achieve some variety in their work.

A Glimpse into the Illustration Process

Most illustrators begin their work by making pencil sketches. Next, they break the story into pieces and decide which parts will be pictures. After that, most of them create a storyboard, or set of sketches for each page.

Where do illustrators get their ideas for books? Just like in writing, illustration ideas come from several places: some from the imagination, many from childhood experiences, some from school visits, and some from their own recent lives. Characters drawn by illustrators are often based on real people. Many illustrators note the influence of nature on their work. And they describe hours of research and reworking.

What Do Illustrators Do?, by Eileen Christelow, is a valuable resource. In the same humorous vein as the author's earlier book, *What Do Authors Do?*, two fictional illustrators go through all the steps involved in creating new picture books. Along the way, readers are introduced to such concepts as layout, scale, and point of view.

Cut-paper Collages

Here are some examples of books that use this technique:

- *Dogzilla*, by Dav Pilkey
  When Dogzilla invades Mousopolis, the rodent citizens must save their city before it gets chewed to pieces. The colorful, collage-style illustrations are full of visual puns.
- *Waters*, by Edith Newlin Chase and Ron Broda
  Share a thrilling cross-country wildlife watching journey.
- *8 O'Cluck*, by Jill Creighton and Pierre-Paul Pariseau

A hungry wolf plans to eat his neighbors, the chickens, for dinner — but they have their own secret plans.

Eventually, they do the final art. Laying out the pages is a challenge. Since readers shouldn't see the same layout from one page to the next, illustrators vary their pages. Some pages have two or three "scenes," others have no words, and some pages are all words. Illustrators change the perspective too. Sometimes, they'll do a close-up of a character, or show a scene as if the reader were looking at it from above or below.

Once all the pages are done, the book goes to the publisher to check that everything is in order. Then it goes to the printer. Soon it is printed, bound, and ready to read!

Illustrating in the Classroom

Explain to your students that most illustrators make many sketches before doing their final artwork, as well as storyboards.

Brenda Clark, the illustrator of the Franklin the turtle books, exemplifies this approach. First, she does a storyboard. She carefully reads the story that Paulette Bourgeois has written and decides what words make good pictures. Then, she does little pencil sketches of how each page could look so that nothing gets left out and nothing gets repeated. Sometimes, she makes several storyboards before she is ready to go on to the next stage. After she's finished that process, Clark makes actual-size sketches of each page, then paints the pictures.

Suggest that children make storyboards for their books. You can use *Helping Kids Draw & Write Picture Books*, by Emily Hearn and Mark Thurman, to teach this exciting approach. Another wonderful classroom resource is Rhian Brynjolson's *Art & Illustration for the Classroom*. It offers a wealth of teaching techniques, including how to use storyboarding and illustration as companions to the writing process.

Illustrating with paper is another option. A self-taught paper sculpture artist, Ron Broda created striking illustrations for *Have You Seen Bugs?*, *Waters*, and *Dinosaur: Digging Up a Giant*.

Collage illustrations have much to recommend them, too. Pierre-Paul Pariseau has won many awards for his unique ones. The cut-and-paste technique he used in *8 O'Cluck* is called photomontage. Images were collected from magazines, catalogues — things lying around the house.

Understand that not everyone likes to draw. That's why the technique of collage, where different materials are cut and pasted to a surface, is an excellent alternative for some children. To show a forest, for example, they can use bits of real shrub for tree branches and pieces of felt to create animal fur. Offer your students choice, and encourage them to explore various illustration techniques.

Encourage your students to study pictures and draw from their strengths. Examining artwork is an excellent way to improve students' artistic skills. With time and practice, their own special style will develop, enabling them to truly enhance their published work.

13

Designing Publishing Projects

"Direct children to thoughtful writing and exciting illustrations . . . encourage them to consider design as an essential feature of original picture books."

— Mark Thurman, in *Helping Kids Draw and Write Picture Books*

So, your students are in the throes of making books. They've got all their ideas and have written them out in rough. Now, they'll need to start considering the design of their publishing projects. With ideas from this chapter, you can help them produce all kinds of great-looking — and readable — children's books.

Designing Page Layouts

Study several picture books with children, highlighting the different types of page layouts. In some books, such as *Chin Chiang and the Dragon's Dance*, by Ian Wallace, the pictures are on separate pages to illuminate the text. In other books, such as *Franklin in the Dark*, by Paulette Bourgeois and Brenda Clark, text and illustrations are equally important and totally integrated. Several variations appear below.

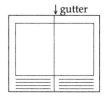

double-page spread

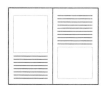

text and pictures alternate

six small pictures with sentences under each one

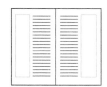

pictures on each side, with text down the middle

Encourage children to focus on variety. Tell them to choose a picture book, such as *The Balloon Tree* which includes all of the preceding layouts, and slowly turn each page, "reading" the illustrations instead of the text. Recommend that they try these layouts when making their own books.

Here are some suggestions on developing effective page layouts.

- For a double-page spread, be careful that nothing important ends up in the crack. Generally, you'll want to keep the gutter, which is the space closest to the centre of an open book, free.
- Allow plenty of space for headings and make the print large enough to be read easily.
- Remember to indent paragraphs in the text. Text without indents slows reading speed.
- Plan white space for your pages. Adequate margins at top, sides, and bottom rest the eye and prevent that crowded appearance which makes reading a strain. Usually, the bottom margin is biggest.
- Allow for sufficient leading, the spacing between lines of type. The eye has difficulty finding the next line if the spacing is inadequate. The simplest thing to do for a school project is to double-space.

Even before the illustrator begins laying out pages, a key design decision has been taken — the shape of the book. Will it be upright, like *Something from Nothing*, or landscape, like *Two by Two*? The vertical shape of *Something from Nothing* ideally suits the depiction of the subtext, showing how the mice use scraps of blanket, underneath the main story. The horizontal shape of *Two by Two* reflects the long ocean journey taken by Noah in his Ark. Students must determine which shape best suits their book content.

Hand-Size Books

The size of a book is often determined by the reader's age. For instance, small books are best suited to preschoolers because they are easier to handle. Similarly, a large storybook, which is more difficult for a small child to hold, is conducive to a shared reading between adult and child. If your students are making board, pop-up, lift-the-flap, and rhyme books for preschool or Kindergarten children, they should ensure that the book size is proportionate to the size of the children's hands.

Lettering

Some students find lettering the most exciting part of their projects. Explain to them that the style of lettering should suit the subject or mood of the book. Thick, heavy type can drown a light, delicate picture. A slight typeface can make the artwork overpowering. Ornate letters can sometimes frustrate readers. The placement of type over, under, next to, or separate from the picture is a deliberate design decision.

Letters may be big or little, fat or thin, plain or fancy. They may even look like the object they name. For titles, some letters look better when they are cut out of colored paper or gift-wrap and glued to the cover. Remind students to use a ruler and draw guidelines to keep their letters even and well spaced.

Creating headings

Playing with Letters

Here are a few ideas for novelty headlines.

- Instead of drawing letters, try other techniques: use a stencil, or cut the letters out of fabric or paper.

- Think of images and textures that suit your subject: for example, you might use water droplet shapes for rain and furry letters if the subject is animals.

- In lieu of a heading, just design the first letter of the first word in a new piece of text, perhaps making it more ornate and larger than the rest of the text.

A heading, or title at the head of a page or section, is meant to capture and focus the reader's attention. It conveys a message about the content through its boldness, style, and contrast with the body text. The nature of various headings reflects their relative importance: type is probably bigger and bolder for major headings and smaller for minor headings. Invite your students to take a look at how some designers treat headings. Children's non-fiction titles are good places to start.

It's easy to create stylish headings with computers! Fancy letters are fun, especially when they suit the story. Headings can be distinctive — as long as they are readable. Typefaces come in a broad range of categories, including handwriting, script, business, holiday, and calligraphy. Older students love to experiment with fonts, which are sets of letters, numbers, and symbols of a given size and design. Remind students to offset headings with white space.

Having fun with fonts

There is now a phenomenal selection of fonts to choose from, but legibility should always be the main criterion in the choice of type. There are basic differences between typefaces. The most common letters used in publishing are those with serifs, or cross strokes at line endings.

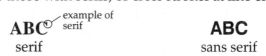

ABC — example of serif

serif

ABC

sans serif

More modern-style typefaces without serifs are described as sans serif. Serif faces are generally more readable than sans serif ones, so encourage your students to use them for body text. Both serif and sans serif faces are good for headings and captions.

Most faces are available in a slanted version known as italic which can be used for emphasis, notes, and captions. Usually, the upper limit for type in adult books is 12 points, or one-sixth of an inch. Books for children are often set in larger sizes.

Common Typefaces

Serif:

Baskerville	Aa Bb Cc Dd Ee Ff Gg Hh Ii Jj Kk
Bodoni	Aa Bb Cc Dd Ee Ff Gg Hh Ii Jj Kk
Century	Aa Bb Cc Dd Ee Ff Gg Hh Ii Jj Kk
Garamond Antiqua	Aa Bb Cc Dd Ee Ff Gg Hh Ii Jj Kk
Goudy	Aa Bb Cc Dd Ee Ff Gg Hh Ii Jj Kk
Souvenir	Aa Bb Cc Dd Ee Ff Gg Hh Ii Jj Kk
Times Roman	Aa Bb Cc Dd Ee Ff Gg Hh Ii Jj Kk

Sans Serif:	
Helvetica	Aa Bb Cc Dd Ee Ff Gg Hh Ii Jj Kk
Optima	Aa Bb Cc Dd Ee Ff Gg Hh Ii Jj Kk
Univers	Aa Bb Cc Dd Ee Ff Gg Hh Ii Jj Kk

Borders

For a special touch, some illustrators add borders to offset their pictures. Usually, they choose a border that corresponds with the story. Point out to your students various border treatments that you see in books. A perfect example is Jan Brett's *The Night before Christmas*, in which the illustrator adds extra stories in the intricate borders. Other Jan Brett books with borders include *The Mitten* and *The Hat*. Marc Brown always creates a border on the cover of his Arthur books. Can your students find other borders?

Explain to your students that a border can be used to frame a complete page, to highlight a special part of it, or just to underline a heading. Once they have seen several examples in books, encourage them to create borders in their own projects.

There are many kinds of borders, many of which can look neat without the use of a ruler. Borders can be as simple as a wavy line or as complex as the carefully researched nautical knots in Phoebe Gilman's *Grandma and the Pirates*. They can even be made from shoelaces, ribbon, or fabric! *Rhinos for Lunch and Elephants for Supper*, a Maasai tale retold by Tololwa Mollel and illustrated by Barbara Spurl, provides a model for creating a colorful geometric border. Students can design something similar by selecting items from a tray of assorted geometric shapes. Or, they can practise printing borders, using small spools, wood-molding scrap, or sponges dipped in paint.

Special Pages for Publishing Projects

Point out to students examples of "special" pages in a few of the books you read to them. The pages that most apply to students are the title, dedication, and copyright ones.

Title Page: A page near the beginning of a book lists the title, author/illustrator, and publishing house with logo. It may also feature an illustration.

Dedication Page: Authors and illustrators often dedicate their books to someone special or to someone who has helped them along the way. Dedications are usually placed on the back of the title page.

Copyright Page: A copyright notice which states the year of publication and the name of the author/illustrator can go at the bottom of the same page as the dedication.

Invite children to look through other books to find examples of these features and to note where they appear. Encourage children to incorporate these details into their own books.

The author page

Finally, we come to those wonderful words — About the Author and Illustrator. Here, students get a chance to describe themselves. They may mention hobbies and activities, as well as include a photo which will add interest for the reader. Children may also want to tell why they chose the subject of their book. Author pages make students feel important. Above all, they should have fun writing about themselves!

Close-up on Covers

"You can't judge a book by its cover." Or can you? We all do! If a cover grabs us, we'll look more closely. Explain to your students that if they want people to read their work, they've got to give it an exciting cover.

Where do cover ideas come from? For picture books, publishers wait until all the illustrations are done. Often, one of those pictures is ideal for the cover. Occasionally, artists create a special image that expresses the feeling of the story without giving too much away. For novels, publishers choose scenes they think have a strong visual impact in the story. Then editors, artists, and marketing staff brainstorm ideas for covers and titles. They keep suggestions coming, no matter how outrageous they may seem, until everyone agrees on one great idea. Recommend that your students wait until near the end of the publishing process for cover and title ideas.

What makes a good cover? It takes an eyecatching image, a strong title treatment, and a striking design to make it happen. Front covers should contain the title of the book, an illustration, and the name of the author/illustrator. The cover sums up a book in one glance.

Choose at least five books to show your students. Discuss with them which covers are well designed and which poorly designed. Have them point out the strengths and weaknesses of each cover. Here are some key elements of well-designed front covers:

- The title is easy to read and interesting to look at.
- Large bold letters make up the title and smaller letters, the name of the author/illustrator. All front cover elements should be big and bold enough to read from a distance.
- The cover illustration reflects the subject of the book.
- All elements come together as a pleasing whole.

Once students understand the basic criteria for designing good book covers, there's more they can do! Here are some suggestions to help make their publishing projects look exciting and different.

Made to Measure

If you have access to a scanner or a photocopier, you have flexibility. If a child's author photo — or illustration — is too small, just enlarge it to the right size. Or, if the original is too big, reduce it until it's the size desired.

Support Your Students' Creative Side

Designing covers offers students excellent experience in "packaging" a product. Avoid using covers where wallpaper is glued over cereal-box cardboard. Promote those that are especially created by children!

- Add interest by pasting pictures onto colored shapes.
- Use contrast — dark letters on a light background or light letters on a dark background — so that letters show up well.
- Consider adding a fancy border.
- Cut, fold, and glue paper together to create a three-dimensional effect. Covers don't have to be flat!
- Work with textured items that relate to the topic. For example, glue pasta onto a colorful background for a project on Italy or food.
- Tear cover edges for an interesting effect.

Tell students not to overlook a book's back cover. It may contain information and a picture of the author/illustrator, or an illustration, or reviews of the book. Explain to your students that publishers usually send copies of their books to newspapers, special journals, and magazines so that reviewers will read them and then write comments; sometimes, they obtain comments by influential people before publication to add to the back cover.

Many Authors, One Designer

If you create a cooperative class book, choose one student to design the cover and attach it to the book.

Binding the Book

As students move into the binding phase of book making, they will need a large table to assemble their pages. Set up an area in the class, or arrange to use the library or a multipurpose room. Remind children to check that their pages are in the correct order.

> **Four Easy Methods of Attaching Pages**
> 1. Simply staple pages together.
> 2. Glue each page to a backing of construction paper, then staple.
> 3. Fold each page in half, then glue back to back.
> 4. Fold each page, then stitch down the centre.

There are other book binding options for your students to consider. They can use ribbon or cloth to bind pages together. Or, if available, a cerlox-binding machine works well. Finally, an alternative to binding at the side is to glue, staple, or sew pages along the top edge.

Hand in hand with book binding is the process of laminating. If you want to protect your students' books, particularly if they're going to be added to your library collection, mount the covers on sturdy paper and laminate them.

What about fun formats?

Consider experimenting with a variety of fun formats: shape books, accordion books, lift-a-flap books, pyramid books, pop-up books, and more. David Kehoe's *Story Presentations* is an excellent source of information on this subject. It offers oodles of unique presentation formats supported by step-by-step instructions.

So, beyond writing stories, students need to consider book design which complements the text. Here they have opportunities to experiment with such elements as layout, lettering, covers, and borders. Challenge children to produce books that readers will find attractive and inviting.

14

Evaluating Student Publishing

Evaluations made in everyday life are often hastily formed subjective opinions and gut feelings. Making an evaluation in teaching, however, requires more than a gut feeling. It requires an objective opinion, based on a set of formal standards.

Objectivity is the key to evaluation in any subject area, including writing and art. Evaluations promote growth and excellence. If a student excels in certain areas, say so! Similarly, constructive comments will help students learn how to improve their work.

When it comes to writing, the purpose of evaluation is to help students write more effectively. Use evaluation both in diagnosing students' strengths and weaknesses and in judging the success of the program. That will help you report to parents in a clear, precise way.

Your role in evaluation is to make positive comments which will help children grow as writers. Students can then incorporate useful advice into the writing. As they write more competently, students can assume more responsibility for evaluating their work.

Evaluation Techniques for Publishing

Throughout this book we have touched on evaluation as it relates to publishing. Here are four evaluation techniques that can strengthen the success of your publishing program.

Portfolios

Just as professional writers and illustrators keep portfolios of their work, your students can keep samples of their writing and illustrations in a folder (a file folder, large envelope, or scrapbook). As a reflection of proven ability, a folder offers one means of assessing their learning. Let students select their own samples, or choose them yourself. When children choose their favorite writing, pictures, and projects to add to their portfolios, ask them to give reasons for their decisions. Remember to date each sample. By examining a portfolio, you can refresh your memory about a student's progress and decide what areas may need improvement.

Conferences

Conferences are a good way to provide students with individual help. Just as an author meets with an editor to discuss new pieces of writing, the student and teacher should meet periodically to discuss current work. The teacher's role is to help rather than criticize. Leading questions such as "Can you think of another way to say . . ." allow students to focus on their strengths and weaknesses. Examine their writing in general terms and in view of objectives previously set. Then decide whether or not to add new objectives to the list.

Teacher's comments

Comments on a student's work should be brief and clear. Concentrate on things the writer has done well and on the student's message. Always use a positive tone when you make suggestions for improvement. Your written comments should serve as a model of effective writing that is easily understood by the student.

Checklists

Making a checklist is useful because it helps clarify skills, habits, and attitudes towards learning. Once each term, complete a checklist like the one on page 123 for each of your students, basing your assessment on what you observe in the classroom.

Making Formal Evaluations

Formal evaluation involves a three-step process, outlined below:

1. Describe the object of your evaluation (for example, the publishing project).
2. Set up a list of standards. (See Publishing Project Evaluation.)
3. Compare the object of your evaluation to the list of standards.

These three steps apply to any evaluation you make and are useful for marking a publishing project. Be sure to clarify the expectations with your students before they begin their projects.

Publishing Evaluation Checklist

	Frequently	Sometimes	Seldom	If "Seldom," explain
1. Invests time and effort in the project				
2. Rough work (sketches, notes, drafts) indicate concepts are being mastered				
3. Meets project requirements				
4. Arrives at solutions to problems				
5. Work shows progress over year				
6. Transfers skills in lessons to other areas				
7. Works well independently				
8. Works well in a group				
9. Demonstrates writing ability				
10. Demonstrates creativity				
11. Works carefully				
12. Uses time wisely				
13. Profits from incidental learning				

Publishing Project Evaluation

Name _____ Date_____

Project _____

The following rating scale is based on the expectations listed below.

1 — Unsatisfactory   2 — Below expectations   3 — Meets expectations
4 — Exceeds expectations   5 — Outstanding

1. *Ideas and Development:* The project follows a logical order. It has a beginning and an ending. Ideas are presented clearly.

    1   2   3   4   5

2. *Sentence Structure:* Ideas are presented in complete sentences.

    1   2   3   4   5

3. *Punctuation:* Capital letters and punctuation are used appropriately.

    1   2   3   4   5

4. *Spelling:* Words appropriate to grade level are spelled correctly.

    1   2   3   4   5

5. *Vocabulary:* Words are used to convey meaning.

    1   2   3   4   5

6. *Visuals:* Visuals are neat and show detail.

    1   2   3   4   5

7. *Ability to Follow Directions:* Directions given for the project were followed.

    1   2   3   4   5

8. *Research:* There is evidence of research and/or knowledge of subject.

    1   2   3   4   5

9. *General Appearance:* The project is neat and complete.

    1   2   3   4   5

10. *Creativity:* The project shows unique or inventive thinking.

    1   2   3   4   5

Score: 20 – 29 points = 73 – 79 percent
           30 – 39 points = 80 – 89 percent
           40 – 50 points = 90 – 100 percent

Mark: _____

Comments: _____

_____

_____

_____

Making a Good and Fair Assessment

Evaluations may contain both praise and criticism. Aim to produce an evaluation that is a constructive balance of the two.

To make a fair assessment, follow the three steps outlined above. Keep ongoing records of a student's performance. Make notes each week or each month so that you will have a complete picture at the end of the year.

Many teachers say that evaluation is the most difficult aspect of their job. You can improve your own evaluation skills by using the three-step method. The next time you assign a publishing project, practise describing the assignment, setting up a list of standards, and comparing each project to the list.

15

Celebrating the Publishing Process

"When the books are done, *have a publishing party.* We do, so should they. In a festive atmosphere of food and drink, streamers and balloons, invited parents and guests, a justly rewarding formality may be established for the proceedings . . . This is the time for sharing books."

— Mark Thurman, in *Helping Kids Draw and Write Picture Books*

You've published books in your class — now what? How will they be shared? Should they be read aloud, displayed in the classroom, given as gifts, taken home, or filed in portfolios?

Considering the effort that goes into making a book, celebrating the finished product is one of the most important parts of publishing. Many teachers prepare displays of children's work, host Family Reading Nights, and help organize Young Authors Conferences for their students. Much more than isolated events, these occasions are part of a cohesive publishing program. They help to promote positive attitudes about writing and offer wonderful ways to recognize students for their good work and creativity.

Use these ideas as building blocks, or adapt them to suit your needs.

Sharing in Groups

Students can share their writing with others in several ways. You can divide the class into groups of three to five students and have the members of each group read aloud their published work. You can arrange for students to read their work to the whole class or to another class in the school. You can also see that projects are exchanged with another class in the school.

Displays of Student Work

One of the most powerful motivators for children is seeing their own work on display. Show children's writing and illustrations on bulletin boards whenever possible. You can also display student projects in the library, front foyer, school board office, fairs, and other community exhibits.

A variation on the display idea is the "one-person show." Just as authors and illustrators often have a show to launch a new book or to exhibit original work, provide opportunities for students to have shows featuring their writing and artwork.

Planning Special Events

Planning is the key to success for any special event. Whether you are organizing a Family Reading Night, Young Authors Conference, or any other activity, you must consider the needs of those involved — teachers, students, parents, and speakers. Here are some planning guidelines.

- Identify the event's goals. These goals will guide your design and implementation of the event, to ensure the proper tone for it.
- Use floor plans to determine the parameters for your planning.
- Consider what will attract guests, then design the event so that everyone can see, hear, and enjoy the activities.
- Script the event to account for all action, minute by minute, including setup, the program itself, and removal of equipment.
- Establish contingency plans. What happens if a guest speaker is late? Determine who will decide to implement the contingency plan and how it will be communicated to others.

Family Reading Nights

Family Reading Nights are festive events at which the guests of honor are children's authors and illustrators. After children make brief presentations of their own in the gym, families attend small group sessions with authors and illustrators. During the evening, children mingle and share books with parents.

Consider Family Reading Nights as a great alternative to spring concerts. They convey a positive message about literacy and are a big hit with parents. Host one, perhaps in Education Week, and thereby enable children to display and share their publishing projects.

First, decide whether your Family Reading Night will involve the entire school or just one division. If you teach in a big school, consider hosting a Family Reading Night with the Junior division one year and the Primary division the next year. Then, estimate how many people you expect. The key is to keep it simple and well organized. Here's how:

Acrostic Poems

With the class, make a list of favorite authors and illustrators. Choose one name from the list, and print each letter of the name on a piece of cardboard. Beside each letter, write a word or phrase that begins with the letter and that is related to the name. The last line must also serve as an ending. For example:

Easy to read
Remarkable
Imaginative
Cricket lover

Caterpillar lover
Artist
Resourceful
Loves nature
Engaging

1. Choose a fun theme, for example:

   pigs — "Pig Out on Books"
   dragons — "Reading Is Hot Stuff"
   pirates — "Hooked on Books"
   mysteries — "Take a Closer Look"

2. Have each class make up a brief presentation on the theme to perform for parents. Children might present a simple rap, rhyme, song, or an acrostic poem, taking about three minutes per class. (The dramatization of an entire book would take too long!) *Student presentations are key to parent attendance.*

3. Ask parents and children to rotate to smaller group sessions with the children's illustrator and author, and ensure that everyone gets a chance to curl up and read books on display in the library.

4. Give each family a Book Bag containing bookmarks, posters, and reading information to take home.

OR

1. Display published work in the gym, where families can congregate to share published projects.

2. Arrange for a master of ceremonies to welcome everyone and introduce special guests, then ask families to rotate to smaller group sessions.

Sample of a Family Reading Night agenda

6:00	Set up display and activity areas.
6:30 – 6:45	Welcome. Families enter gym. Presentation by hosts and children
6:45 – 7:45	Rotation of three groups
Workshop A:	Meet the author. Location: Kindergarten
Workshop B:	Meet the illustrator. Location: Lunchroom
Workshop C:	Time to read books. Location: Library
7:45	Children and parents return to gym to collect Book Bags.

Family Reading Night countdown plan

Three Months Before

✓ Strike an organizing committee consisting of an administrator, a librarian, and a teacher.

✓ Establish how the event will be funded.

✓ Decide on date, time, and grade levels involved.

✓ Brainstorm ideas for presenters (e.g., one author and one illustrator).

Two Months Before

✓ Submit permit for using the building, if necessary.

✓ Select and contact presenters.

✓ Choose theme for event (perhaps from works of the author or illustrator).

✓ Choose a master of ceremonies.

✓ Contact publishers, public library, and local bookstore by phone to request their participation.

✓ Follow up with letters and maps to publishers and presenters.

✓ Request Book Bag donations.

✓ Notify staff of event, goals, and theme.

✓ Announce event in school newsletter.

One Month Before

✓ Contact media (local television, newspaper, radio).

✓ Book Bag donations are collected and stored.

✓ Provide detailed announcements in school newsletter.

✓ Arrange videotaping. Obtain advance permission from presenters.

Two Weeks Before

✓ Prepare class presentations to open the evening. Keep them simple!

✓ Decide on decorations. Have a decor group coordinate, collect, put up, and take down decorations.

✓ Organize Junior/Intermediate helpers to act as hosts, greeters, parking lot attendants, etc.

✓ Confirm booking with media.

✓ Send invitations to special guests such as the mayor, trustee, consultants, and director of education.

One Week Before

✓ Send a letter of invitation to participating families. Explain the format of the event. Include an agenda and tear-off portion of letter for parents planning to attend.

✓ Order refreshments.

Three Days Before

✓ See that Book Bags are collated by student helpers.

✓ Provide reminder of event on P.A. system (perhaps note home to parents).

✓ Have staff promote enthusiasm for the evening.

On the Big Day

✓ Staff divides students into three groups.
✓ Furniture setup is complete.
✓ Post welcome signs, footprints, balloons, etc.
✓ Decorations are in place.
✓ Book Bags are ready to be distributed.
✓ Hospitality area (staffroom) is set up.
✓ Brief hosts on welcoming procedures (assisting guests, use of nametags).

Follow-up

✓ Signs and decor are taken down.
✓ Ensure all rooms are back in order.
✓ Send thank-you letters to participating presenters/exhibitors.
✓ Share children's and parents' responses.
✓ Share success of evening in next newsletter.
✓ Acknowledge contributions of staff and students on P.A. system.

Actual attendance is one measure of a successful event. Another measure is how participants feel about the event, and whether or not they talk about it in a positive way. One principal sums up her school's first Family Reading Night in this way: "The evening itself was a delight. About 75 kids and parents attended readings in the classrooms, while about 150 with their own books were at the gym. The real value rested in the goodwill. Everyone seemed appreciative of the effort."

Young Authors Conferences

Many schools hold a Young Authors Conference, or Writers' Conference, to honor children's publishing. Professional authors, illustrators, newspaper editors, cartoonists, and storytellers come to share their expertise and see the children's work. These professionals encourage children, as a future generation of writers, to work at their writing skills. Just as a sports meet is an occasion to honor athletes, a Young Authors Conference allows student writers to read each other's work and gather for a day's discussion of writing.

Young Authors Conferences can involve individual schools or families of schools. A conference is preceded by months of planning by organizers, and weeks of publishing activity in the classrooms of participating teachers. The in-school conference is planned by a group of teachers and parents for all students and teachers. The district conference is planned by a committee of teachers for students who possess a keen interest in writing and/or illustrating. All students will have created books.

A district conference is usually held in a high school, local auditorium, school board office, or public library. The number of participants determines the amount of space needed.

Here are some aims for a Young Authors Conference:

to promote writing within the classroom;
to encourage the publishing of student writing;
to foster the concept of sharing student work with peers; and
to inspire students by providing guest authors and illustrators.

Sources of funding for a Young Authors Conference vary. A school-level conference may receive financial support from a parent-teacher organization, book fair fundraising, and other fundraising efforts. District-level conferences are usually subsidized by reading councils and teacher associations.

The format of the conference depends on the event's scale. Essentially, the agenda should allow for students to share their writing with one another, and for them to meet and hear presentations from professionals in the book business — writers, illustrators, storytellers, and poets.

Suggested Conference Format

1. Greetings: Opening remarks by designated speakers
2. Large group session given by poet, storyteller, author, or illustrator
3. Refreshment break — juice and cookies
4. Mini-workshops (see suggestions below)
5. Sharing of books: Children share portions of their books or their whole books with small groups.
6. Closing ceremonies: Thank-yous, certificates given out, closing remarks

Ideas for mini-workshops

Not only do Young Authors Conferences honor publishing successes, but students gain inspiration and knowledge to apply to future projects. Students are divided into groups of eight to ten. Group members share their books and take part in mini-workshops led by teachers, parent volunteers, and people from the publishing business. Students choose which sessions they want to attend before the conference day.

Ideas for mini-workshops include the following: Storyboarding, Scanning Basics, Lettering Fun, Fun Strategies for Revising, Career Awareness, Researching on the Internet, Editing ABCs, Cartooning, Creative Collage, and Once upon a Puppet!

The key reason for undertaking any of the activities outlined in this chapter is to recognize students for the writing that they do. Ultimately, publishing is an excellent way to motivate students to write well. Knowing that their work will be displayed for others to read encourages students to take particular care with a final copy. Revising and editing are time consuming, but the result is generally well worth the effort. Writing and illustrating books stimulate all kinds of creative possibilities which students can explore as they improve their composing skills.

FEATURE: Creative Careers — An Eye to the Future

Do you have a top-notch writer or artist in your class who wants to pursue work in the publishing field, but isn't sure how? Encourage interested students to learn as much as possible about job options. These outlines will help answer important career questions.

A Writer's Career Profile

What Students Who Aspire to Careers in Publishing Can Do

While still in school students can do the following:

- experiment with various forms of writing or art that they are interested in;
- explore a wide range of authors and illustrators to develop a sense of various styles;
- write or illustrate for the school newsletter or yearbook;
- volunteer to work on newsletters for community groups or local newspapers;
- develop a portfolio of work.

Writers research, prepare, and write materials for publications such as newspapers, magazines, books, technical manuals, and trade journals. They work for advertising agencies, governments, consulting firms, and publishing companies, or are self-employed. Most writers need excellent research skills and a solid grasp of writing mechanics.

Nature of the job

Research-based positions include writers of books, speeches, news releases, manuals, brochures, articles, reports, presentations, newsletters, and correspondence. Writers may also be involved with copy editing, proofreading, fact checking, transcribing, and translating.

Creative writers include playwrights, poets, short-story writers, and novelists.

Working conditions

The working environment varies. Writers can work in an office or from their homes as freelancers. Usually writers work under tight deadlines.

Preparation needed

There is no specific path to become a writer. Some people learn on the job; others study journalism, English literature, or corporate communications. The most important thing is ability. All writers keep a portfolio of their work. Necessary skills include above average grammar, attention to detail, strong research skills, a versatile writing style, persistence, and determination.

Remuneration

Generally, writers are paid low salaries. Writers with companies have the benefits of a permanent position whereas freelance writers depend on the size and number of contracts they get. The average author gets 10 percent of the total sales of a book.

Employment forecast

Good writers are always in demand. The use of freelance writers continues to grow. Often though, companies hesitate to use new people and hire those with whom they are familiar. As writers develop their portfolios and reputations, it gets easier to find new projects.

Related careers

Columnist, editor, journalist, magazine writer, publisher, technical writer, and writing instructor

Writers and illustrators often take further courses in areas like editing, copywriting, and desktop publishing. This lets them experiment with new techniques and get feedback from others. Many writers join groups where they exchange work for suggestions and encouragement.

An Illustrator's Career Profile

Illustrators create designs, pictures, cartoons, storyboards, and caricatures for advertising, education, entertainment, and other purposes. They work for advertising agencies, magazines, newspapers, and book publishers.

Nature of the job

Book publishers hire illustrators on a project basis. One book can take months to years to illustrate. Artists work with the editor and author until everyone feels that the pictures suit the story. Opportunities here are fulfilling because they allow artists to really explore their creativity.

Working conditions

This field relies heavily on freelancers. Therefore, most artists work at home, and create an atmosphere that suits their needs. Illustrators usually have many projects to keep them going. In a year they may contribute to a monthly magazine, work for an ad agency, and illustrate a picture book.

Preparation needed

Most illustrators study art at college or university. To be accepted in a post-secondary program, they must submit a portfolio that shows their talent. They need visual awareness and technical skills; the ability to communicate through a variety of media including pencils, pastels, markers, oil paint, watercolor, and charcoal; a broad knowledge of various art forms such as photography and sculpture; and knowledge of computer technology and the printing process.

Remuneration

Usually, picture book illustrators are paid half of the royalties on a book, which are split with the author. Royalties are generally 10 percent of the retail price of the book.

Employment forecast

Knowledge of computer graphics is important, but there will always be a demand for high-quality illustration made by hand.

Related careers

Advertising designer, art director, graphic artist, medical/scientific illustrator, animator

---

Appendix: So, *You* Want to Be a Writer?

Many teachers try their hand at writing a children's story and want to send it to a publisher. Does this sound like you? If so, chances are you've been concentrating on characterization, plot, setting, and style. Maybe you've had someone do the illustrations and others give you feedback. Now, it's time to publish your story, but how?

If you're longing to write a children's story or have already written one, but don't yet have a home for it, that's great! But first, get to know the publishing industry. Understand that book publishing is both a cultural activity and a business. Learn how the industry works, what editors and agents look for, and how to develop a marketing strategy. Keep in mind that writers face stiff competition for the number of books published each year.

You should also know that writing and illustrating children's books does not bring great financial rewards. In fact, writers and illustrators are near the bottom of the economic ladder. No one is in this field to make a lot of money. Most people are in it because they love books, they love kids, and they want to encourage literacy.

Organizations such as the ones listed on pages 39–40 offer loads of information on publishing. These organizations have helped to foster hundreds of authors and illustrators. Budding writers can obtain a guide on the submission process and a list of children's publishers accepting unsolicited manuscripts. To learn everything you can about the publishing industry, consider joining one or two of these organizations. Take courses they offer, attend meetings, and participate in workshops. You may wish to volunteer your services for the sake of networking.

In addition to organizations, the Internet and books offer tips, articles, links, and market information for writers. The following sites are designed to help you get published:

- *Inkspot: The Writer's Resource and Newsletter:*
  http://www.inkspot.com
- *The Slush Pile:*
  http://www.theslushpile.com
- *Tips for Writers:*
  http://www.olywa.net/peregrine/index.html

Bibliography of useful books on getting published

- *Book Publishing: The Basic Introduction,* by John P. Dessauer
- *Writing Picture Books: What Works and What Doesn't,* by Kathy Stinson
- *Nonfiction Book Proposals Anyone Can Write: How to Get a Contract and an Advance before Writing Your Book,* by Elizabeth Lyon
- *The Sell-Your-Novel Toolkit: Everything You Need to Know about Queries, Synopses, Marketing and Breaking In,* by Elizabeth Lyon
- *Writing in a New Convertible with the Top Down: A Unique Guide for Writers,* by Sheila Bender and Christi Killien

Explanatory Notes

The following "publishing" terms are defined simply here. They are intended to help you when working with children in the production of their own books.

ant's eye view the underview of a picture, from the ground looking up

background in art, the part of a composition that appears to be farthest from the viewer

binding stapling, taping, gluing, or sewing of finished pages to make a book

bird's eye view the overview of a picture, from the sky looking down

body type the type used in the main text, excluding headings

boldface heavyweight type (**abc**)

character a person or animal in a story

collage a form of art in which a variety of materials (e.g., pictures, fabric, objects) are glued to a background

copyright a small c in a circle, followed by the year the book was finished and the name of the person who has the legal right to reproduce the material

close-up a picture with a close range view showing the character or scene on a large scale

display type type used for chapter titles and headings, usually larger or bolder than text type

double-page spread a single picture which spreads across two pages

editing the making of changes to the content, structure, and wording of writing to improve the organization of ideas, correct grammar and spelling, and ensure the writing is clear and correct

elements of design essential aspects of art including color, line, texture, and shape

endpapers plain or decorated papers at the beginning and end of hardcover books

font the attributes for a given typeface in a specific size, slant or weight

foreground the area of a picture that appears closest to the viewer

freelancer an artist, writer, editor, etc. who is self-employed and works for various organizations

geometric shape a shape that is based on geometric form (e.g., circle, square, triangle)

gutter a margin adjoining the inside unbound edge of a page

italics slanted version of type (*abc*)

layout the plan of a page, the process of arranging type and illustration on a page

leading spacing between lines of type

logo a symbol that identifies organizations, products, etc.

medium any material used by an illustrator to produce a work of art

ms. manuscript, the original work written by the author and submitted to the publisher

proofreading the careful reading of a final draft to correct errors in grammar, spelling, and punctutation

plot what happens in a story

reference a book, etc. used for information as an aid in research

revising changing the content and/or organization of a draft

rough a sketch or draft done before the final art

royalties share of sales income paid to authors and illustrators, based on the number of copies sold

running heads captions at tops of pages identifying book, parts, or chapters (also, running feet at the bottoms of pages)

sans serif letters without serifs or short strokes at line endings (The)

serifs letters with short cross strokes at line endings (The)

setting where and when a story takes place

shade a color with black added to make it darker

spine the thin end of the book that holds the pages together

storyboard a series of small rough sketches showing the book; a picture plan of the book

story elements the parts of a story including the main theme or topic, plot, characters, and setting

texture in art, the representation of the surface

tint a color with white added to make it lighter

title page the page at the beginning of a book which lists title, author, and publisher

typeface the particular appearance, size, etc. of a printing type

uppercase capital letters

Teacher/Parent Resources

Asher, Sandy, ed. *But That's Another Story: Famous Authors Introduce Popular Genres.* New York: Walker Publishing, 1996.

Bialostok, Steven. *Raising Readers: Helping Your Child to Literacy.* Winnipeg, MB: Peguis Publishers, 1992.

Booth, David. *Guiding the Reading Process: Techniques and Strategies for Successful Instruction in K–8 Classrooms.* Markham, ON: Pembroke Publishers, 1998.

Booth, David, Larry Swartz, and Meguido Zola. *Choosing Children's Books.* Markham, ON: Pembroke Publishers, 1987.

Botrie, Maureen, and Pat Wenger. *Teachers & Parents Together.* Markham, ON: Pembroke Publishers, 1992.

Brynjolson, Rhian. *Art & Illustration for the Classroom: A Guide for Teachers & Parents.* Winnipeg, MB: Peguis Publishers, 1998.

Canadian Children's Book Centre, The. *Families . . . Read Together.* Toronto, ON: The Canadian Children's Book Centre, n.a.

Canadian Children's Book Centre, The. *Picture This! A Celebration of Canadian Children's Book Illustrations.* Toronto, ON: The Canadian Children's Book Centre, 1995.

Canadian Children's Book Centre, The. *The Storymakers. Illustrating Children's Books.* Markham, ON: Pembroke Publishers, 1999.

Canadian Children's Book Centre, The. *Writing Stories, Making Pictures: Biographies of 150 Canadian Children's Authors and Illustrators.* Toronto, ON: The Canadian Children's Book Centre, 1994.

Gertridge, Allison. *Meet the Canadian Authors and Illustrators: 50 Creators of Children's Books.* Richmond Hill, ON: Scholastic Canada, 1994.

Goldblatt, Joe Jeff. *Special Events: The Art and Science of Celebration.* New York, NY: Van Nostrand Reinhold, 1990.

Greenwood, Barbara, ed. *Behind the Story: The Creators of Our Best Children's Books and How They Do It.* Markham, ON: Pembroke Publishers, 1995.

Greenwood, Barbara, ed. *The CANSCAIP Companion: A Biographical Record of Canadian Children's Authors, Illustrators and Performers.* 2d ed. Markham, ON: Pembroke Publishers, 1994.

Greenwood, Barbara, ed. *Presenting Children's Authors, Illustrators and Performers.* Markham, ON: Pembroke Publishers, 1990.

Hart-Hewins, Linda, and Jan Wells. *Better Books! Better Readers!* Markham, ON: Pembroke Publishers, 1999.

Harvey, Stephanie. *Nonfiction Matters: Reading, Writing, and Research in Grades 3–8.* York, ME: Stenhouse Publishers, 1998.

Kovacs, Deborah, and James Preller. *Meet the Authors and Illustrators: 60 Creators of Favorite Children's Books Talk about Their Work.* Richmond Hill, ON: Scholastic Canada, 1991.

Kropp, Paul. *The Reading Solution: Make Your Child a Reader for Life.* Toronto, ON: Random House, 1993.

Phenix, Jo, and Irene Scott-Dunne. *Spelling for Parents.* Markham, ON: Pembroke Publishers, 1994.

Ray, Arlene Perly. *Everybody's Favourites: Canadians Talk about Books That Changed Their Lives.* Toronto, ON: Penguin, 1997.

Stinson, Kathy. *Writing Picture Books: What Works and What Doesn't.* Markham, ON: Pembroke Publishers, 1991.

Trelease, Jim. *The Read-Aloud Handbook.* 4th ed. New York: Viking Penguin, 1995.

Turbide, Diane. "The KidLit Boom." *Maclean's.* December 11, 1995.

Classroom Publishing Resources

Christelow, Eileen. *What Do Authors Do?* New York: Clarion Books, 1995.

———. *What Do Illustrators Do?* New York: Clarion Books, 1999.

Deakin, David, and Gordon Moore. *Looks Great!: Exciting Ways of Presenting Your Projects.* Markham, ON: Pembroke Publishers, 1992.

Hearn, Emily, and Mark Thurman. *Draw and Write Your Own Picture Book.* Markham, ON: Pembroke Publishers, 1990.

———. *Helping Kids Draw & Write Picture Books.* Markham, ON: Pembroke Publishers, 1990.

———. *Illustration Ideas for Creating Picture Books.* Markham, ON: Pembroke Publishers, 1990.

Kehoe, David. *Story Presentations: How to Turn Your Story, Project or Report into Something Amazing.* Markham, ON: Pembroke Publishers, 1997.

Lewis, Amanda. (Collins, Heather, illus.) *Writing: A Fact and Fun Book.* Toronto, ON: Kids Can Press, 1992.

Stinson, Kathy. (Daniel, Alan, and Lea, illus.) *Writing Your Best Picture Book Ever.* Markham, ON: Pembroke Publishers, 1994.

Thurman, Mark. *Fun-tastic Collages.* Markham, ON: Pembroke Publishers, 1992.

———. *How to Plan Your Drawings.* Markham, ON: Pembroke Publishers, 1992.

Winch, Gordon, and Gordon Blaxell. *The Grammar Handbook for Word-Wise Kids: Basic English Grammar, Punctuation and Usage.* Markham, ON: Pembroke Publishers, 1996.

Featured Children's Literature

Allard, Harry. (Marshall, James, illus.) *Miss Nelson Is Missing.* New York: Houghton Mifflin, 1998.

Allinson, Beverly. (Reid, Barbara, illus.) *Effie.* Richmond Hill, ON: Scholastic Canada, 1990.

Asch, Frank. *Ziggy Piggy and the Three Little Pigs.* Toronto, ON: Kids Can Press, 1998.

Bailey, Linda. (Walker, Tracy, illus.) *Gordon Loggins and the Three Bears.* Toronto, ON: Kids Can Press, 1997.

Base, Graeme. *Animalia.* Toronto, ON: Stoddart Kids, 1993.

———. *The Eleventh Hour.* Toronto, ON: Stoddart Kids, 1993.

Bogart, Jo Ellen. (Reid, Barbara, illus.) *Gifts*. Richmond Hill, ON: Scholastic Canada, 1994.

Booth, David. (Reczuch, Karen, illus.) *The Dust Bowl*. Toronto, ON: Kids Can Press, 1996.

Booth, David, ed. (Kovalski, Maryann, illus.) *Dr. Knickerbocker*. Toronto, ON: Kids Can Press, 1995.

Bourgeois, Paulette. (Wilson, Brenda, illus.) *Franklin in the Dark*. Toronto, ON: Kids Can Press, 1986.

Brett, Jan. *The Hat*. New York: Putnam Publishing Group, 1997.

———. *The Mitten*. New York: Putnam Publishing Group, 1996.

———. *The Night before Christmas*. New York: Putnam Publishing Group, 1998.

Carney, Margaret. (Wilson, Janet, illus.) *At Grandpa's Sugar Bush*. Toronto, ON: Kids Can Press, 1997.

Chase, Edith Newlin. (Reid, Barbara, illus.) *The New Baby Calf*. Richmond Hill, ON: Scholastic Canada, 1990.

Chase, Edith Newlin. (Broda, Ron, illus.) *Waters*. Richmond Hill, ON: Scholastic Canada, 1994.

Cleary, Beverly. *Ramona the Brave*. New York: Dell, 1984.

Cole, Joanna. *The Magic School Bus on the Ocean Floor*. New York: Scholastic Inc., 1994.

Collins, Heather. *One, Two, Buckle My Shoe*. Toronto, ON: Kids Can Press, 1997.

Creighton, Jill. (Pariseau, Pierre-Paul, illus.) *8 O'Cluck*. Richmond Hill, ON: Scholastic Canada, 1995.

Crysler, Ian. *Big City/Big Country Counting Book*. Richmond Hill, ON: Scholastic Canada, 1998.

Dabcovich, Lydia. *The Polar Bear Son: An Inuit Tale*. New York: Clarion Books, 1997.

Davis, Aubrey. (Petričić, Dušan, illus.) *Bone Button Borscht*. Toronto, ON: Kids Can Press, 1995.

———. (Petričić, Dušan, illus.) *The Enormous Potato*. Toronto, ON: Kids Can Press, 1997.

———. (Daniel, Alan, and Lea, illus.) *Sody Salleratus*. Toronto, ON: Kids Can Press, 1996.

Davis, Virginia. (Willms, Russ, illus.) *Simply Ridiculous*. Toronto, ON: Kids Can Press, 1995.

Denton, Kady Macdonald. *A Child's Treasury of Nursery Rhymes*. Rev. ed. Toronto, ON: Kids Can Press, 1998.

Doyle, Brian. *Angel Square*. Toronto, ON: Groundwood, 1995.

Dunn, Sonja. *All Together Now*. Markham, ON: Pembroke Publishers, 1999.

Dunn, Sonja. *Primary Rhymerry*. Markham, ON: Pembroke Publishers, 1993.

Ehlert, Lois. *Red Leaf, Yellow Leaf*. San Diego, CA: Harcourt Brace, 1991.

Flack, Marjorie. (Wiese, Kurt, illus.) *The Story about Ping*. New York: Puffin Books, 1993.

Gibbons, Gail. *The Seasons of Arnold's Apple Tree*. San Diego, CA: Harcourt Brace, 1988.

Gilman, Phoebe. *The Balloon Tree*. Richmond Hill, ON: Scholastic Canada, 1984.

———. *Grandma and the Pirates*. Richmond Hill, ON: Scholastic Canada, 1992.

———. *Something from Nothing*. Richmond Hill, ON: Scholastic Canada, 1992.

———. *The Wonderful Pigs of Jillian Jiggs*. Richmond Hill, ON: Scholastic Canada, 1990.

Godfrey, Martyn. *Wally Stutzgummer, Super Bad Dude*. Richmond Hill, ON: Scholastic Canada, 1992.

Hall, Zoe. (Halpern, Shari, illus.) *It's Pumpkin Time!* New York: Scholastic Inc., 1994.

Harrison, Troon. *The Dream Collector*. Toronto, ON: Kids Can Press, 1999.

Hunter, Bernice Thurman. *As Ever, Booky*. Richmond Hill, ON: Scholastic Canada, 1985.

———. *That Scatterbrain Booky*. Richmond Hill, ON: Scholastic Canada, 1981.

———. *With Love from Booky*. Richmond Hill, ON: Scholastic Canada, 1983.

Korman, Gordon. *The 6th Grade Nickname Game*. Markham, ON: Scholastic Canada, 1998.

———. *Beware the Fish!* Richmond Hill, ON: Scholastic Canada, 1980.

———. *The Chicken Doesn't Skate*. Richmond Hill, ON: Scholastic Canada, 1996.

———. *I Want to Go Home!* Richmond Hill, ON: Scholastic Canada, 1981.

———. *Liar, Liar, Pants on Fire*. Richmond Hill, ON: Scholastic Canada, 1997.

———. *Losing Joe's Place*. Richmond Hill, ON: Scholastic Canada, 1990.

———. *Macdonald Hall Goes Hollywood*. Richmond Hill, ON: Scholastic Canada, 1992.

———. *Radio Fifth Grade*. Richmond Hill, ON: Scholastic Canada, 1991.

———. *Something Fishy at Macdonald Hall*. Richmond Hill, ON: Scholastic Canada, 1995.

———. *Son of Interflux*. Richmond Hill, ON: Scholastic Canada, 1995.

———. *This Can't Be Happening at Macdonald Hall*. Richmond Hill, ON: Scholastic Canada, 1980.

———. *The Toilet Paper Tigers*. Richmond Hill, ON: Scholastic Canada, 1995.

———. *The Twinkie Squad*. Richmond Hill, ON: Scholastic Canada, 1994.

———. *Who Is Bugs Potter?* Richmond Hill, ON: Scholastic Canada, 1980.

———. *The Zucchini Warriors*. Richmond Hill, ON: Scholastic Canada, 1996.

Korman, Gordon, and Bernice Korman. *Last Place Sports Poems of Jeremy Bloom*. Richmond Hill, ON: Scholastic Canada, 1996.

Kovalski, Maryann. *Take Me Out to the Ball Game*. Richmond Hill, ON: Scholastic Canada, 1992.

———. *The Wheels on the Bus*. Toronto, ON: Kids Can Press, 1990.

Kusugak, Michael. (Krykorka, Vladyana, illus.) *Arctic Tales*. Toronto, ON: Annick, 1998.

———. (McGraw, Sheila, illus.) *Baseball Bats for Christmas*. Toronto, ON: Annick, 1990.

———. (Krykorka, Vladyana, illus.) *Hide and Sneak*. Toronto, ON: Annick, 1992.

———. (Krykorka, Vladyana, illus.) *Northern Lights: The Soccer Trails*. Toronto, ON: Annick, 1993.

Lesynski, Loris. *Boy Soup*. Toronto, ON: Annick, 1996.

———. *Ogre Fun*. Toronto, ON: Annick, 1997.

Little, Jean. *From Anna*. Toronto, ON: HarperCollins Canada, 1972.

Lottridge, Celia Barker. (Wallace, Ian, illus.) *The Name of the Tree*. Toronto, ON: Groundwood, 1989.

———. (Wolsak, Wendy, illus.) *Ticket to Curlew*. Toronto, ON: Groundwood, 1992.

Mackay, Claire. *Mini-Bike Rescue*. Rev. ed. Richmond Hill, ON: Scholastic Canada, 1991.

Martin, Jr., Bill, and John Archambault. *Knots on a Counting Rope*. New York: Henry Holt & Co., 1997.

McGowan, Chris. (Broda, Ron, illus.) *Dinosaur: Digging Up a Giant*. Toronto, ON: North Winds Press, 1999.

McGugan, Jim. (Kimber, Murray, illus.) *Josepha: A Prairie Boy's Story*. Red Deer, AB: Red Deer College Press, 1994.

Mollel, Tololwa M. (Glass, Andrew, illus.) *Ananse's Feast: An Ashanti Tale*. New York: Clarion Books, 1997.

———. (Morin, Paul, illus.) *The Orphan Boy*. Toronto, ON: Stoddart Kids, 1995.

———. (Spurl, Barbara, illus.) *Rhinos for Lunch and Elephants for Supper*. Toronto, ON: Stoddart Kids, 1994.

Munsch, Robert. (Martchenko, Michael, illus.) *50 Below Zero*. Toronto, ON: Annick, 1986.

———. (Martchenko, Michael, illus.) *Alligator Baby*. Richmond Hill, ON: Scholastic Canada, 1997.

———. (Martchenko, Michael, illus.) *Andrew's Loose Tooth*. Markham, ON: Scholastic Canada, 1998.

———. (Martchenko, Michael, illus.) *Angela's Airplane*. Toronto, ON: Annick, 1983.

———. (Askar, Saoussan, illus.) *From Far Away*. Toronto, ON: Annick, 1995.

———. (Daniel, Alan, and Lea, illus.) *Get Out of Bed!* Toronto, ON: Scholastic Canada, 1998.

———. (Martchenko, Michael, illus.) *I Have to Go!* Toronto, ON: Annick, 1987.

———. (Martchenko, Michael, illus.) *Jonathan Cleaned Up, Then He Heard a Sound or Blackberry Subway Jam*. Toronto, ON: Annick, 1981.

———. (McGraw, Sheila, illus.) *Love You Forever*. Toronto, ON: Firefly, 1986.

———. (Duranceau, Suzanne, illus.) *Millicent and the Wind*. Toronto, ON: Annick, 1984.

———. (Martchenko, Michael, illus.) *Mortimer*. Rev. ed. Toronto, ON: Annick, 1985.

———. (Suomalainen, Sami, illus.) *Mud Puddle*. Toronto, ON: Annick, 1996.

———. (Martchenko, Michael, illus.) *The Paper Bag Princess*. Toronto, ON: Annick, 1981.

———. (Martchenko, Michael, illus.) *Pigs*. Toronto, ON: Annick, 1989.

———. (Fernandes, Eugenie, illus.) *Ribbon Rescue*. Toronto, ON: Scholastic Canada, 1999.

———. (Martchenko, Michael, illus.) *Something Good*. Toronto, ON: Annick, 1990.

———. (Martchenko, Michael, illus.) *Stephanie's Ponytail*. Toronto, ON: Annick, 1996.

———. (Martchenko, Michael, illus.) *Thomas' Snowsuit*. Toronto, ON: Annick, 1985.

Munsch, Robert N., and Michael Kusugak. (Krykorka, Vladyana, illus.) *A Promise Is a Promise*. Toronto, ON: Annick, 1988.

Oppenheim, Joanne. (Reid, Barbara, illus.) *Have You Seen Birds?* Richmond Hill, ON: Scholastic Canada, 1986.

———. (Broda, Ron, illus.) *Have You Seen Bugs?* Richmond Hill, ON: Scholastic Canada, 1996.

Paré, Roger. *A Friend Like You*. Toronto, ON: Annick, 1989.

Patterson, Heather. (Gerber, Mary Jane, illus.) *Thanks for Thanksgiving*. Richmond Hill, ON: Scholastic Canada, 1998.

Perlman, Janet. *Cinderella Penguin*. Toronto, ON: Kids Can Press, 1994.

———. *The Emperor Penguin's New Clothes*. Toronto, ON: Kids Can Press, 1994.

Pilkey, Dav. *Dogzilla*. San Diego, CA: Harcourt Brace, 1993.

Prelutsky, Jack. *It's Snowing! It's Snowing!* New York: Greenwillow, 1984.

Reid, Barbara. *First Look* nature series. Toronto, ON: HarperCollins, 1998.

———. *Fun with Modeling Clay*. Rev. ed. Toronto, ON: Kids Can Press, 1998.

———. *The Party*. Richmond Hill, ON: Scholastic Canada, 1997.

———. *Sing a Song of Mother Goose*. Richmond Hill, ON: Scholastic Canada, 1998.

———. *Two by Two*. Richmond Hill, ON: Scholastic Canada, 1997.

———. *Zoe* series. Toronto, ON: HarperCollins, 1991.

Service, Robert. (Harrison, Ted., illus.) *The Cremation of Sam McGee*. Toronto, ON: Kids Can Press, 1986.

Service, Robert. (Harrison, Ted. illus.) *The Shooting of Dan McGrew*. Toronto, ON: Kids Can Press, 1998.

Scieszka, Jon. (Johnson, Steve, illus.) *The Frog Prince, Continued*. New York: Puffin, 1994.

———. (Smith, Lane, illus.) *The Stinky Cheese Man and Other Fairly Stupid Tales*. Toronto, ON: Penguin, 1999.

———. (Smith, Lane, illus.) *The True Story of the Three Little Pigs*. New York: Viking Penguin, 1989.

Slavin, Bill. *The Cat Came Back*. Toronto, ON: Kids Can Press, 1995.

Stinson, Kathy. (Lewis, Robin Baird, illus.) *Big or Little*. Toronto, ON: Annick, 1983.

―――. (Lewis, Robin Baird, illus.) *Red Is Best*. Toronto, ON: Annick, 1982.

Wallace, Ian. *Chin Chiang and the Dragon's Dance*. Toronto, ON: Groundwood, 1984.

White, E. B. *Charlotte's Web*. New York: HarperCollins, 1990.

Yee, Paul. *Tales from Gold Mountain: Stories of the Chinese in the New World*. Toronto, ON: Groundwood, 1989.

Featured Children's Non-Fiction

Bartholomew, Alan. (Bartholomew, Lynn, illus.) *Electric Gadgets and Gizmos: Battery-powered Buildable Gadgets That Go*. Toronto, ON: Kids Can Press, 1998.

Bourgeois, Paulette. (Terlson, Craig, illus.) *The Amazing Dirt Book*. Toronto, ON: Kids Can Press, 1990.

―――. (La Fave, Kim, illus.) *In My Neighbourhood* series. Toronto, ON: Kids Can Press, 1993.

Bowers, Vivien, (Newbigging, Martha, illus.) *Crime Science*. Toronto, ON: Owl Books, 1997.

Drake, Jane, and Ann Love. (Collins, Heather, illus.) *The Kids Cottage Games Book*. Toronto, ON: Kids Can Press, 1998.

Duplacey, James. *Champion Defencemen*. Toronto, ON: Kids Can Press, 1997.

―――. *Hockey's Hottest Centers*. Toronto, ON: Kids Can Press, 1999.

―――. *Hockey's Hottest Defensemen*. Toronto, ON: Kids Can Press, 1999.

―――. *Hockey's Hottest Goalies*. Toronto, ON: Kids Can Press, 1999.

―――. *Hockey's Hottest Wingers*. Toronto, ON: Kids Can Press, 1999.

Greenwood, Barbara. (Collins, Heather, illus.) *Pioneer Crafts*. Toronto, ON: Kids Can Press, 1997.

―――. (Collins, Heather, illus.) *A Pioneer Story*. Toronto, ON: Kids Can Press, 1994.

Gryski, Camilla. *Boondoggle*. Toronto, ON: Kids Can Press, 1993.

Heller, Ruth. *Many Luscious Lollipops: A Book about Adjectives*. New York: Putnam Publishing Group, 1998.

―――. *Merry-Go-Round: A Book about Nouns*. New York: Putnam Publishing Group, 1992.

Hickman, Pamela. (Shore, Judie, illus.) *The Jumbo Book of Nature Science*. Toronto, ON: Kids Can Press, 1996.

Mastin, Colleayn O. (Sovak, Jan, illus.) *Newest & Coolest Dinosaurs*. Calgary, AB: Grasshopper Books, 1997.

Acknowledgments

Over the years, I have had the privilege of working with a number of talented authors, illustrators, and colleagues in the children's book industry. They have supported me in my work and provided me with great insight into the creative process. As well, many excellent teachers have shared teaching strategies and project ideas.

Special thanks go to the following organizations and individuals: my editor, Kate Revington; the staff of The Canadian Children's Book Centre; Barbara Reid; Gordon Korman; Sonja Dunn; Kathy Stinson; Antonietta Giannetta at Tumpane Public School, Toronto District School Board; Leanne McMillan at St. Marguerite d'Youville School, Simcoe Muskoka District Catholic School Board; Karen Hartling and Sandy Moher at St. Luke School, Dufferin-Peel District School Board; Victor Levin, School Services of Canada; Sandi Snetsinger and Jane Anderson at Sir John A. Macdonald School, Durham District School Board; Jane Franklin, Durham District School Board; and Deborah Watson at Cundles Heights Public School, Simcoe County District School Board.

Last but not least, I thank my family and friends for their help and encouragement. As I have plugged away at this, my first book, my husband Jim has filled many domestic holes. Raising my son Cory has given me greater understanding towards children, and changed my life forever. To all, I am profoundly grateful.

Index

5161